Math

GRADES 4–6

Homework

THAT COUNTS

Math Homework

GRADES 4–6

THAT COUNTS

Annette Raphel

MATH SOLUTIONS

SAUSALITO, CALIFORNIA, USA

Math Solutions
150 Gate 5 Road
Sausalito, CA 94965
www.mathsolutions.com

Library of Congress Cataloging-in-Publication Data
Raphel, Annette, 1949–
    Math homework that counts : grades 4–6 / Annette Raphel.
      p.   cm.
    Includes bibliographical references.
    ISBN 0-941355-27-6
      1. Mathematics—Study and teaching (Elementary)   2. Homework.   I. Title.
QA135.5 .R295 2000
372.7'044—dc21

                                         00-040187

    ISBN-13: 978-0-941355-27-8

Appendix E, General Research Findings About Homework, is reprinted with permission from *Homework As a Learning Experience: What Research Says to the Teacher*, 3d edition, by Mary Anne E. Doyle and Betsey S. Barker (Washington DC: NEA Publications, 1990).

The Twelve Days of Christmas has been adapted with permission from the December issue of *Arithmetic Teacher*, copyright 1993 by the National Council of Teachers of Mathematics. All rights reserved.

Editor: Toby Gordon
Copy editor: Alan Huisman
Production: Alan Huisman
Cover and interior design: Catherine Hawkes, Cat & Mouse Design
Cover illustration: Leslie Evans
Composition: Cape Cod Compositors, Inc.

Printed in the United States of America
13 12 11 10 09   ML   4 5

A Message from Math Solutions

We at Math Solutions believe that teaching math well calls for increasing our understanding of the math we teach, seeking deeper insights into how children learn mathematics, and refining our lessons to best promote students' learning.

Math Solutions shares classroom-tested lessons and teaching expertise from our faculty of professional development instructors as well as from other respected math educators. Our publications are part of the nationwide effort we've made since 1984 that now includes

- more than five hundred face-to-face professional development programs each year for teachers and administrators in districts across the country;
- annually publishing professional development books, now totaling more than seventy titles and spanning the teaching of all math topics in kindergarten through grade 8;
- four series of videos for teachers, plus a video for parents, that show math lessons taught in actual classrooms;
- on-site visits to schools to help refine teaching strategies and assess student learning; and
- free online support, including grade-level lessons, book reviews, inservice information, and district feedback, all in our *Math Solutions Online Newsletter*.

For information about all of the products and services we have available, please visit our website at *www.mathsolutions.com*. You can also contact us to discuss math professional development needs by calling (800) 868-9092 or by sending an email to *info@mathsolutions.com*.

We're always eager for your feedback and interested in learning about your particular needs. We look forward to hearing from you.

mathsolutions.com

CONTENTS

This collection of assignments started out not as a book but as homework ideas that I adapted and invented to feed the enthusiasm of the children I teach. I have taught for a quarter of a century and, in every school in which I have worked, have had the incredible luck to encounter children who have largely shared my fascination with mathematics and who have been willing to take risks and think out loud.

My debt to each one of the students I have taught is great. Many of them are now in college, and I still have work of theirs filed away because it represents extraordinary understanding and innovative thinking. My students have made me recognize that children are much more interesting and capable than my college course work led me to believe.

Laura Choate and Patsy Kantor, mathematics curriculum authors and special friends, have joined me in countless conversations about mathematics and teaching and have validated my own enthusiasm for mathematical thought. Pat Davidson became my math therapist for a year (the University of Massachusetts thought she was advising an independent course in their Critical and Creative Thinking program). Gordon Clem, Manon Charbonneau, and Bob Lawler, my teaching colleagues at the annual Dana Hall Summer Math Institute, enhance and broaden my understanding every time we talk. Carolyn Damp, Connie Dodes, Scott Ford, and Paula Rosen regularly invite me into their classrooms and appreciate me enough to give me honest feedback about what is and isn't working.

Derek Stolpe is that rare administrator whose support is extraordinary and unwavering. Donald Duncan, who began teaching the year I was born, has been an unparalleled mentor, pushing my own mathematics understanding and serving as an indelible role model. The friendships of Bob and Weezie Gilpin, Linda Stikeleather, and Phil Sullivan are treasured and rare.

My mother, who was not a college graduate until I was, is a terrific role model, a woman who loves mathematics and who insists on remaining a learner. My father's unconditional support and admiration are an inspiration.

In many ways this book began in New Orleans, where I gave a presentation at a National Council of Teachers of Mathematics convention. Marilyn Burns came to listen (I stopped breathing, thankfully temporarily, when I saw her) and followed up with a phone call. Instead of correcting my fragile differentiation between permutations and combinations, she offered me a professional opportunity as a Math Solutions consultant that has changed my life. Her books have given me the information and courage to teach for understanding, and her mentorship has been inspiring. My Math Solutions colleagues and I teach and learn from one another; we share stories about our schools, the children we teach, and the other teachers on our faculties. I cannot possibly give adequate thanks for these personal and professional friendships.

Toby Gordon initially influenced me by her thoughtfulness in getting the first great math education books on the market in her previous role as math editor at Heinemann. As the editor of this book, she had to make house calls to get ideas out of folders and into a manuscript.

My husband, Steve, who was a mathematics major when we met, is my primary cheerleader and tutor. His interest in the world of mathematics piques my own, and his ability to clarify difficult concepts has rescued me more times than I care to admit. His intelligence and humor are as important to me now as they were when we were still in college. My son Aaron, currently an engineering student, showed me how much a child could be enchanted by mathematics. My son Jordan, a seventh grader, has field-tested many of these ideas at our dining room table. One of these sons did his homework largely without me, the other challenged my optimism about the benefits of homework. I won't tell you which child matches which description; suffice it to say I have experienced both ends of the spectrum!

Were you to move from one city's school system to another or even from one school to another in the same system, you would probably find a different curriculum, a different environment, and different expectations. But, more than likely, you would find homework.

Three groups of people have a big stake in homework—teachers, parents, and students. Unfortunately, they all have different perspectives on the subject. As in the story of the blind mice who examine different parts of an elephant and come to different conclusions (see Ed Young's *Seven Blind Mice* for an example of this ancient tale), we all look at homework quite differently. Not surprisingly, it's the rare homework assignment that meets everyone's goals.

An article by Jianzhong Xu and Lyn Corno (1998a) crystallizes much of the murky tension surrounding homework. Roughly half of the teachers these researchers consulted believe that the major reason homework is given is to reinforce what is being learned in school: the school day simply isn't long enough, and homework is an opportunity to extend what students are learning. Teachers also believe that homework develops a sense of responsibility in children. (I identify with these attitudes, although I hope the potential of homework is broader than that of simply reinforcing my lesson plans.) The parents these researchers surveyed agree that homework reinforces school learning, both by deepening understanding and integrating new learning. However, they feel that one of homework's greatest purposes, regardless of how painful, is to help their children be independent. (The current spate of articles by parents about their unwanted, unexpected, and unrewarding roles as homework partners provides an ironic counterpoint here!) Parents see learning how to do homework as an important prerequisite for success in life and later schooling. (Hmm! I identify with that as well.) The children Xu and Corno spoke with report that they think homework is assigned to help them understand better what they have learned in class: if they do their homework, they will learn more, write better, and "do math better." They feel another major reason for doing homework is that it is important to their parents and their teachers. (Seeking adult approval is a big deal for children.)

Since parents, teachers, and children direct somewhat different lenses toward homework and voice different reasons for doing it, it's no wonder homework is controversial. How can homework simultaneously fulfill all these missions? And how do we begin to evaluate the worth and success of homework if we are using three different sets of criteria?

Since homework creates tension in so many homes, I've synthesized a list of ways that have been suggested for parents to help their children with homework (Appendix A: What You Can Do to Help Your Child With Math Homework This Year). You may want to share this list with the parents of your students or generate one of your own based on the aptitudes, styles, and temperaments of the children in your classroom. Additional appendixes list the characteristics of good homework, highlight the variables associated with homework, suggest questions teachers should ask about their homework assignments, summarize research findings regarding homework, suggest resources for math homework ideas, and direct you to suppliers of math education materials.

Our practice needs to be informed by research but also by experience. It is in that spirit that I share examples of the homework I have assigned and my students' often remarkable responses. I offer here a repertoire of problems and experiences that have managed to intrigue children and garner the interest of their parents. All the assignments were made in upper elementary classrooms—grades 4, 5, and 6—and are geared toward mathematical discovery.

The National Middle School Association suggests that there are four categories of homework: assignments geared toward practice, assignments that prepare students for upcoming lessons, extension assignments that require abstract thinking skills, and creative assignments that encompass many skills and ideas. I found these categories particularly useful and have organized this book around them, devoting a chapter to each category.

The first time I tried many of these activities, they did not yield the kind of mathematical thinking I had hoped for. Tinkering with ideas is as important as adjusting ingredients in a recipe. These lessons should be tailored to your class, your curriculum, your temperament, and your interests. They are meant to whet your appetite for what is possible, to inspire you, and to reaffirm the importance of teaching. Encouraging children to think in inquiring, creative, and critical ways as they enter their second decade will give them the firm foundation of computation and number sense they need.

Math
Homework
as
Practice

1

2

3

4

I remember it, and I suspect you do too. Tucked into the book bag or under an arm was a textbook. The homework assignment was to do all the problems on two consecutive pages. After the first couple of problems, the remaining dozen or so were a snap. But if the first problem or two didn't make sense, the hour ahead loomed bleak and hopeless.

Not only do I remember doing this kind of homework, I remember assigning it! Oh, I may have individualized my worksheets somewhat and run them off on one of those purple mimeo machines, but the idea was essentially the same: give students lots of practice in whatever computational skill we were currently learning in class. Those who understood could work on automatic pilot, applying the algorithm with rigid and successful precision. Those who couldn't get it, whether conceptually or mechanically, faced a night of torture, one in which a frustrated parent often "helped" with shortcuts or instructions that fostered neither understanding nor proficiency.

Indisputably, practice is important. Revisiting what you know is imperative in building a solid foundation. If you can't do arithmetic, you can't successfully problem solve. If you don't know what 5×6 is, you won't be able to extrapolate what 50×600 or $.5 \times 60$ is. It's that simple. Unfortunately, many of today's "progressive" mathematics teachers give the impression that they care more about problem solving than arithmetical proficiency. The truth is, you won't be able to do the former without having the latter.

Everyone who wishes the math standards in America were higher has the same goal. The real debate is how best to gain this arithmetical proficiency. Some really fine mathematicians assume that because drill and rote practice led to their own current expertise, this is the sure and only way to make arithmetic automatic. And I am realistic enough to acknowledge that my own experiences are with a small, finite population of children and that my methods may not apply equally to other schools. However, what the children I teach have been learning, thinking, and applying is too exciting not to share and suggests a viable alternative route to computational facility.

What I am advocating here is not that we abandon repetition altogether but that we use it judiciously to enhance understanding. There are good reasons for this (see Hiebert and Carpenter 1992):

1. *Understanding generates more understanding.*

2. *Understanding promotes recall.* Constructing understanding is not passive, and the structures that help us comprehend material also help us remember it. Rules stored as isolated pieces of information are much more difficult to retrieve than rules embedded in a broader understanding.

3. *Understanding reduces the information that must be remembered.*

4. *Understanding enhances the transfer of information from one context to another.*

5. *Understanding influences beliefs about mathematics.* Students who are asked only to memorize procedures think that mathematics is mainly a matter of following rules, that it consists mostly of symbols on paper, and that the symbols and rules are disconnected from other things they know about mathematics.

Example Activities

Numbers on a Pathway

SOURCE: adapted from Clark and Carter 1988

This activity can be a very effective homework assignment after it has first been introduced in the classroom. The object is to throw two dice (one standard, the other a special one containing the numbers 4 through 9) to create two-digit numbers, then place the numbers in a series of ten circles, ordering them from smallest to largest. The number on either die can be used in the ones place, with the remaining number then used in the tens place. For example, if you throw a 4 and a 9, you can make a 94 or a 49. Once a number has been placed in a circle, it can't be moved to another. If a throw of the dice doesn't produce a number that will fit on an empty circle in the pathway, the game continues but a tally needs to be recorded. The goal is to complete the pathway without having to record any tallies, something not easy to do.

The first thing I discovered was that children wanted to add the two numbers, a natural result of having played board games in which the numbers on a pair of dice are added to determine how far a player can advance her or his token. The next thing I realized was that although my directions were clear to me, they weren't necessarily clear to my students. I decided that we would first play a game together as a class.

On my fourth-grade-classroom chalkboard I drew ten circles, marking the first one *start* and the last one *finish*. I told the students these were stones in a pathway, to underscore the idea of progression. I also had two dice, a standard one marked with pips (1 through 6) and a special one marked with the numbers 4 through 9. (I made the special die with a color cube and some oval self-stick labels on which I had written the numbers, drawing a line under the 6 and the 9 so that we could tell which was which.)

My first throw was a 4 and a 7. I asked what two-digit numbers could be made using those numbers, and the children easily identified 47 or 74.

"I know," Julia said, "since there are ten stones in the pathway and there are ten tens in a hundred, we could figure out where to put numbers that way. We could put 47 in the fourth oval 'cause that will be for the forties."

Danny said, "Yeah, but wait a minute. What could we put in the first stone? We won't have any numbers less than ten. The numbers have to have two places. Wait a minute! We can put a number that begins with one in that first stone. The first number [digit] will be the number of the stone it is in."

I clarified Danny's explanation for the rest of the class. "So a number in the thirties, which begins with a three, will be in the third stone, and a number in the seventies, which begins with seven, will be in the seventh stone." I then asked, "Well, what is the smallest number we could possibly make with these two dice?"

There was a flurry of talking. Colin blurted out, "Eleven."

"Nah," said Ibbie. "That can't happen with these dice. There isn't a one on both of them, Colin."

Danny raised his hand. He was one of the dependable thinkers in the class, and I hesitated before calling on him, because I wanted the other children to have some time to think. However, I appreciated his kindness toward his classmates and his charitable way of explaining things in a way that didn't make them feel inadequate. Finally I nodded for him to comment. "There is a one on the regular dice," he said, "But the smallest number that is on the other special dice is a four. So I think fourteen is the smallest number possible."

I asked whether anyone had a different idea or whether they all agreed with Danny. The consensus was that his explanation seemed to make sense. We then figured out that 96 was the largest possible number. Finally, we put the 47 in the fourth stone, as Julia had suggested.

The next throw was a 5 and a 6. Using our previous reasoning, we put the 56 right after the 47.

I wondered whether any of the children would notice that some digits were more likely to appear than others or figure out that some numbers were impossible to form.

A 5 and a 7 followed. There was general agreement that we should put the 75 in the seventh stone. Would anyone notice that there would be an extra stone if we kept following our strategy? In mathematics we often stick doggedly to algorithms (set procedures), and one of my goals as a teacher is to model that we always need to think about numbers, whatever procedures we happen to be following. I decided I would introduce a new idea before we committed ourselves. "I think we should at least consider putting a 57 in the stone next to the 56," I said. "What do you think?"

There was a somewhat stunned silence as the children considered this threat to their earlier comfortable conclusion. Then Seth said, "I think having two numbers next to each other means that you have bigger space for other numbers."

I waited. It's hard to wait, even though we all know that research shows it is important. Katie said, "Maybe you think some numbers will be more popular than others?"

"What do you mean?" I prodded.

"Well, I noticed that even though we have rolled only three times, numbers in the middle keep coming up. We haven't put anything on the end stones."

There was a quiet murmur. "Well," I asked, "*are* any numbers more likely to come up?"

Emma, who rarely gets excited about math, waved her hand wildly. "There is a four, five, and six on both of the dice, so they will come up the most."

"It will be harder to get numbers not in the middle," Katie added. "You know, like a one or a two or an eight or a nine."

Danny said, "So when we get one of those numbers, we should be sure to use it. If we get a five and a one we should make fifteen, not fifty-one."

"We can't make fifty-one now anyhow, because it doesn't have a stone to go on," Zack pointed out.

The class decided that since 5 and 7 were both middle numbers (not differentiating between the 5, which is on both dice, and the 7, which is only on one), they would stick with their original plan and put the 75 in the seventh stone. So much for teacher intervention. Our path now looked like this:

The next roll was a 4 and a 4. "Hey," said Nolen, "we don't get a choice of what number to make. That's not fair." We talked about doubles, and how we would have no choice with 44, 55, or 66.

"The good news," said Nia, "is that we can put the forty-four in front of the forty-seven. The bad news is, that's our stone for numbers in the thirties." We updated the pathway:

Next we rolled a 3 and a 9. The class decided to put a 93 at the end of the pathway, although a few children wanted to reserve that spot for 96, the largest possible number. This exasperated the children who had figured out that getting a 9 and a 6 together was unlikely. (Children approach any lesson with very different levels of number sense.) The deciding factor seemed to be A.J.'s comment that if we got a 9 and a 6 we could always make 69. There was still room for that. So now we had:

The 2 and 8 we rolled next went into the second stone, though that would not have been my choice:

The next roll, a 3 and a 5, stopped us short. Neither 35 nor 53 would fit. We reluctantly put a tally mark in the upper right-hand corner of the chalkboard. "What numbers," I wondered out loud, "would be impossible to get with these two dice?"

It dawned on some of the children for the first time that not all the numbers between 14 and 96 were possible. Someone suggested that double-identical-digit numbers were impossible, but then we realized that three of these numbers—44, 55, and 66—were possible. In fact, we had gotten and were able to use 44. However, numbers with zeroes in them were impossible; single-digit and triple-digit numbers were impossible; and numbers in which both digits were small or large—89 or 21, for example—were impossible. Now we had three categories of numbers to think about: those that were possible, those that were more likely, and those that were impossible. This was a lot of mathematics to consider.

A 6 and a 5 came up next, and there were several moans, because we'd had that combination before. But Maddie immediately saw that we had room for a 65, so we put it in the sixth stone:

"It's really hard to get numbers on the sides," observed Colin. "Our middle is all filled in."

Ibbie said, "That's because numbers in the middle are more likely to come up. When we play this again, I think we should try to fill in the ends first and not worry so much about whether a number that begins with a five is in the fifth stone."

A 7 and a 6 appeared next, and 76 slipped in neatly after the 75:

It didn't matter that we didn't really have two choices (a 67 would have nowhere to go), since one fit where we wanted it. Also, most children didn't seem to be bothered that the increments between numbers were not regular, that between some numbers there was only a difference of one, while others were more than ten numbers away from their nearest neighbor.

I was worried about the probabilities of filling in the last two stones. "Let's figure out what we would like our next roll to be," I suggested. We decided a 1 on the standard die with any other number would be fine with us. A 2 on that die with a 4, 5, 6, or 7 would work well too. We needed an 8 on the nonstandard die with anything on the standard die, or a 9 on the nonstandard die with a 1 or a 2 on the other one. All and all, there were eighteen different possibilities that would work. With older students, this would also be a great time to talk about the total number of possible rolls (14 through 19, 24 through 29, 34 through 39, 41 through 49, 51 through 59, 61 through 69, 71 through 76, 81 through 86, 91 through 96, for a total of 63 possibilities) and the probability of turning up what you need (in this case, 18 out of 63, or about a 28 percent chance).

When the next throw was a 1 and a 9, I was amazed. The combination would fit in either space. If I had had a chance to think about the problem as leisurely as I'm writing about it (and in the same quiet and with the same focus), I would have encouraged the children to put it in the eighth stone, since there were eight possible throws of the dice that would work there and ten possibilities that would work for the first stone. But when you stand in front of a class, you are tuned in to the children, not necessarily to mathematical intricacies. Besides, it is wonderful to bring the same intuitive wonder to a problem that your children have, rather than a studied answer. One of the reasons it behooves us to try any suggestion, lesson, worksheet, or game at home before we teach it and to reflect on a lesson afterward by writing about it is that it builds our own mathematical understanding. If your experience in college was anything like mine, you were far better prepared to teach reading than mathematics. I need lots of time and experience to improve my own understanding of mathematics, even the math I teach to young children. By the same token, I think my interest (rather than my expertise) in mathematics has been responsible for some of the enthusiasm I model as I try new lessons. Suffice it to say, we put 19 in the first stone:

Then we had a string of impossible rolls, 5 and 2, 4 and 1, and 4 and 4. Finally, an 8 and a 5 turned up, and we triumphantly placed 85 in the remaining stone (the ninth) and counted up our four tally marks. Our finished pathway looked like this:

You can't plan your rolls, of course, but I was grateful that we did not get through the pathway without some unusable ones, since I wanted the students to know it was unlikely they would make it through without any tally marks.

After this demonstration game, the students played a number of rounds on their own with randomly assigned partners. (I assign partners by dealing out cards; students with equivalent cards in the same-color suit—red threes, black queens, etc.—become partners.) Two pairs of students actually had tallyless pathways. I think it's important not to play games like this competitively but to work together toward a common goal. I also want my students to verbalize their strategies and articulate their positions, so I establish a class culture in which thinking out loud is acceptable and doing so is encouraged.

The next day we did the pathway activity again, this time with three dice (two standard ones, one special one with the numbers 4 through 9) and thirteen stones. We figured out that the smallest three-digit number we could get would be 114 and the largest would be 966. This version was easier in some ways (there was a wider span of numbers) and harder in others (with three different digits, there were often six possible numbers to consider!). That night I sent each child home with a plastic baggie containing three dice. For homework they could play either version of the game and had to write about some of their strategies and things they discovered.

There are a number of reasons why the pathway activity is a good homework assignment:

1. It doesn't look like standard homework; a baggie full of dice is a lot different from a textbook or a worksheet.

2. It is open ended; asking children what they notice allows for a wide variety of expertise and engages them regardless of their level of mathematical understanding.

3. It is social. Parents enjoy playing the game and are able to see what the school values in mathematics in the context of a shared recreational and intellectual mathematical experience. The tensions associated with a frustrating homework assignment are avoided.

4. It incorporates many strands of mathematics. Children do some basic thinking about probability, explore the logic of various strategies, consider

permutations of numbers involving the same digits, and solidify their understanding of place value.

5. It subtly says that mathematics can be engaging as well as rigorous.

6. It allows children to be the experts as they explain to their parents, siblings, caretakers, etc., what the task is and why they feel certain moves are strategically sound.

7. There is no one right answer, which counteracts the mistaken impression many students have that mathematics means arithmetic with exactly one right answer. However, it becomes clear that certain strategies work better than others.

8. The common experiences children have playing the game lead to rich conversations about their discoveries, triumphs, and disasters and expose them to one another's thinking. The source of mathematical expertise shouldn't always be the teacher.

9. It encourages children to think about larger numbers as a whole, not just in terms of their individual digits.

10. It fulfills the January 1985 *Harvard Education Newsletter*'s recommendations for homework assignments: it is short, the materials are provided, and students are sure to experience some measure of success.

Rethinking Worksheets

Although I have discovered the power of giving children blank paper on which to organize their thinking and long ago abandoned the notion that worksheets I set up are always the most efficient way for children to think about mathematics, there are times when a worksheet is appropriate. I don't condemn all of them. But there are good worksheets and not-so good ones. Good worksheets embed computational practice in a problem-solving format.

Dr. Lola May, who writes books about mathematics education and speaks often on the topic, makes a tongue-in-cheek suggestion to single out certain categories of problems on a worksheet. "Don't bother doing the whole thing," she brashly suggests you tell your students, "just do the problems which have even answers, or the ones where you have to borrow when you subtract. Just do the two problems that have the greatest and least answer on the page. Just do the problems where there are exactly two digits in the answer." This is a great technique. The children think they are getting away with murder, as they cheerfully tally up all of the problems for which they are no longer responsible. I am gleeful because I know that in order to complete my assignment, they have to think about every problem on the page, strengthening their number sense, in order to decide which problems actually fit the criteria I have given them. They will discover the conditions under which a sum is even, which require regrouping, or which will produce more or fewer digits in an answer.

Figures 1.1–1.4 are examples of worksheets that I think are terrific. I never photocopy a worksheet protected by an active copyright. I want to demonstrate my respect for the copyright laws and for authors' work and thus instill this attitude in my students. Therefore, I adapt or "tweak" them in some way—include fewer examples,

FIGURE 1.1   *A Good Worksheet*

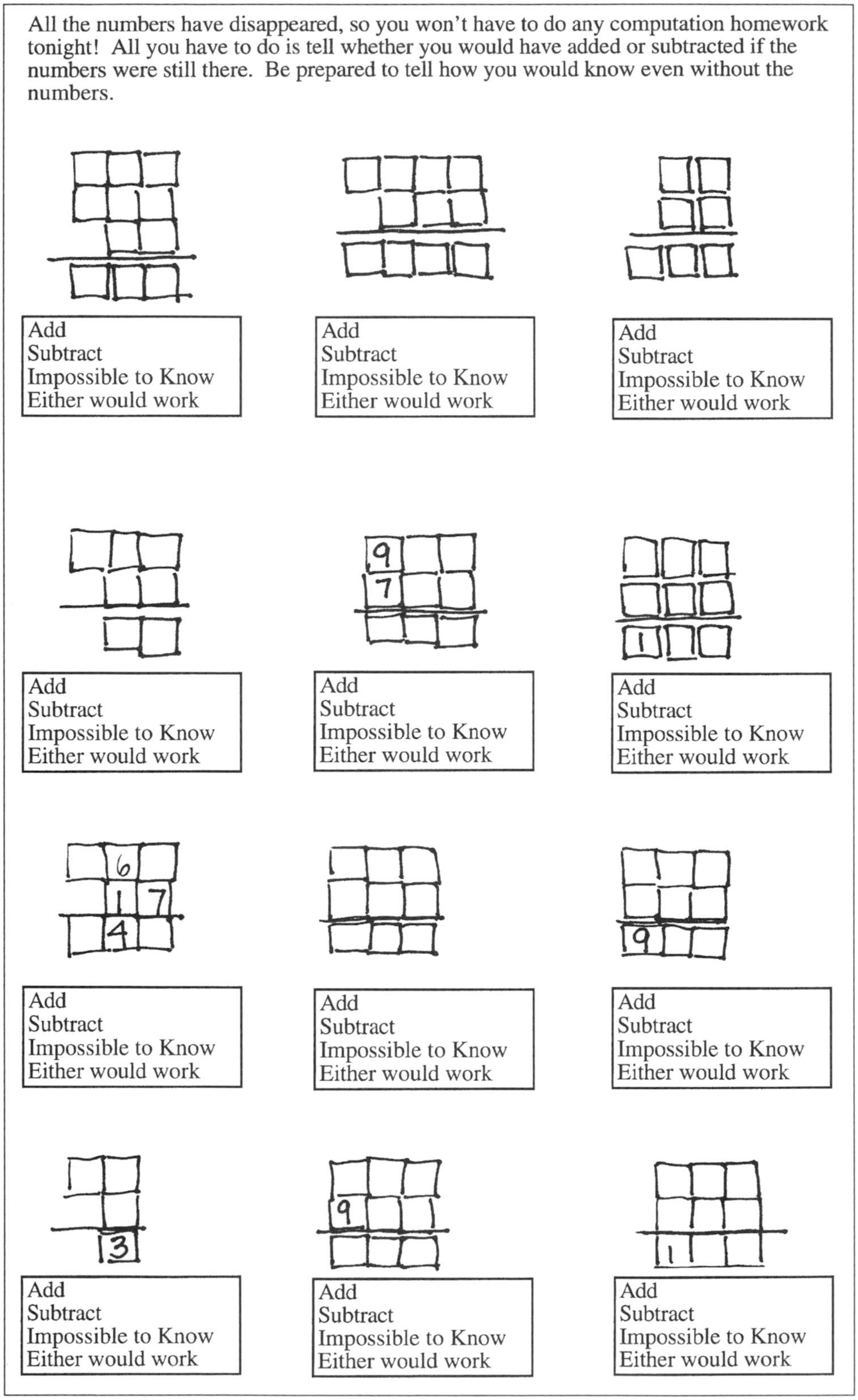

All the numbers have disappeared, so you won't have to do any computation homework tonight! All you have to do is tell whether you would have added or subtracted if the numbers were still there. Be prepared to tell how you would know even without the numbers.

Add
Subtract
Impossible to Know
Either would work

Add
Subtract
Impossible to Know
Either would work

Add
Subtract
Impossible to Know
Either would work

Add
Subtract
Impossible to Know
Either would work

Add
Subtract
Impossible to Know
Either would work

Add
Subtract
Impossible to Know
Either would work

Add
Subtract
Impossible to Know
Either would work

Add
Subtract
Impossible to Know
Either would work

Add
Subtract
Impossible to Know
Either would work

Add
Subtract
Impossible to Know
Either would work

Add
Subtract
Impossible to Know
Either would work

Add
Subtract
Impossible to Know
Either would work

FIGURE 1.2 *Another Good Worksheet*

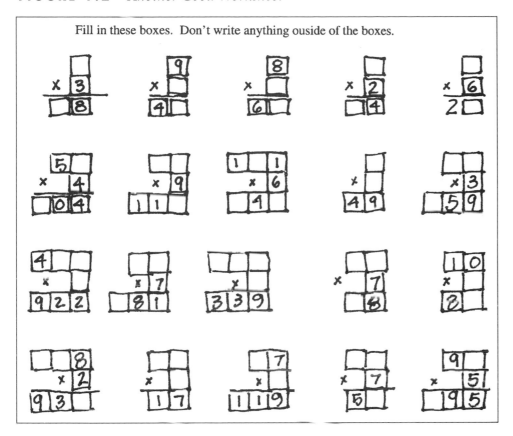

make the numbers harder or easier, change whole numbers to decimals, whatever. Although this is extra work, children and parents appreciate receiving worksheets that are obviously mine, and I get to tailor them for the children I am teaching.

Before I began writing this section, I spread out some good worksheets in front of me and determined some general criteria for what made them good:

1. A good worksheet should be mathematically rich. There are cute or clever activities that do not push mathematical thinking. A worksheet that asks for simple regurgitation will teach neither the children who have difficulties nor those who have already mastered that skill. This is the core criterion, and it is absolutely necessary; nevertheless, it is not sufficient in itself.

2. A good worksheet should be interesting. Although there is no guarantee that a group of children will all find the same things interesting, a worksheet has to look different enough from a textbook or from a bunch of computationally equivalent problems to pique interest. That being said, figure 1.2 may look, at first glance, like traditional computational practice, but I believe a closer look will convince you (and your students) that it pushes arithmetic understanding to the problem-solving level.

3. A good worksheet should stimulate connections. Either the mathematics should cross strands (link geometry and number sense, for example, or computation and measurement), or it should connect mathematics with literature, the real world, or another discipline.

FIGURE 1.3   *Still Another Good Worksheet*

Decimals

Put decimal points in four different ways to make four
number sentences which are true

1 4 6 × 3 1 2 = 4 5 5 5 2

1 4 6 × 3 1 2 = 4 5 5 5 2

1 4 6 × 3 1 2 = 4 5 5 5 2

1 4 6 × 3 1 2 = 4 5 5 5 2

Don't bother figuring out the answer, just tell me how many
digits are in the whole number part of the decimal

$3\overline{)43.5}$ ___ $.9\overline{)11.7}$ ___

$1.7\overline{)399.5}$ ___ $.2\overline{)8.3}$ ___

$.023\overline{).4117}$ ___ $28.3\overline{)3281.668}$

$4.5\overline{)25056}$ ___ $.98\overline{)448.84}$ ___

Pick 2 numbers. Record them.   Add them. If the
answer is between 0–20, get 1 point. If the answer is between
20 and 40 get 2 points. If the answer is between 40 and 60
get 3 points. If the answer is between 60 and 80 get 4 points.
Total your points after 3 rounds. How did you do?

Numbers to choose from
32.7   19.8   40.16   4.38   .86   52.1   3.8
7.41   .03   61.7   29.4   5.7   9.78   4.4

                                                     points   Grand total

Round 1   ___   +   ___

Round 2   ___   +   ___

Round 3   ___   +   ___

FIGURE 1.4 *One More Good Worksheet*

TANGRAMS

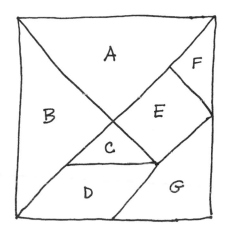

Fractions and Geometry:
If the whole square is worth one then....
1) Use C and ___ to make a square worth 1/8
2) Use E, ___, and ___ to make a triangle worth 1/4
3) Use A and ___ to make a triangle worth 1/2
4) Use pieces ___, ___, and ___ to make a triangle worth 1/4
5) Use pieces ___. ___. and ___ to make a square worth 1/4
6) Use pieces ___, ___, ___, and ___ to make a triangle worth 1/2
7) Use ___, ___, ___, and ___ to make a rectangle worth 3/8

Numerical Reasoning and Geometry:
If A and B = $12.00 each, G = $10, C and F = $3, E = $6, and D = $8 then
1) Can you use three pieces to make a $12 isosceles trapezoid
2) Make a $24 parallelogram
3) Make a $14 rectangle
4) Make a $38 parallelogram
5) Use five pieces to make a $30 square
6) Make a $26 square
7) Make a $22 trapezoid

4. A good worksheet should be rooted in problem formulation, problem solving, and/or mathematical reasoning. Given the finite amount of time we have, any assignment has to push a child's thinking. While I explicitly endorse automaticity of facts, very little else in mathematics should be automatic. The real truth is that the application of mathematics (or anything else, for that matter) requires thinking. And thinking is a habit that can be encouraged by regularly requiring it.

5. A good worksheet should promote communication. After solving problems or filling in information, students need to be asked to reflect on their answers, talk about patterns they notice, explain why something is not possible, or

generate a new problem modeled after those with which they have been dealing. While not all worksheets need a narrative section, arithmetic and linguistic thinking are no longer considered mutually exclusive.

6. A good worksheet should advance student understanding. If we are not asking children to go beyond what they already know by continually encouraging them to increase their capacities as mathematical thinkers, we are not making good use of assignments. One way to advance student understanding is by encouraging metacognition—that is, prompting students to think about what they know and how they know it. A worksheet can take a concept that is supposed to be in a child's repertoire and push it in a way that enhances or deepens understanding. It can help a child see what he already knows with greater clarity, or help her apply it to more complex material.

7. A good worksheet should not be too intimidating. If a worksheet appears too daunting, students may never even begin. A simple rule of thumb is that there must be enough visual "white space" that the student believes it is doable.

8. A good worksheet should not require students to do arithmetic for arithmetic's sake. Any arithmetic should serve a greater purpose: categorizing, sorting, identifying a pattern, developing number sense, understanding.

My friend and colleague Cathy Fossum designs some of the clearest homework assignments I have ever seen (see figures 1.5 and 1.6). She makes sure not only that children are aware of her expectations but also that parents can figure out, at a glance, what is important. She incorporates reflection, assessment, communication, thinking, contexts, and choice. Feel free to use her work as a guide.

FIGURE 1.5A *Cathy Fossum's True Stories Homework*

Table #_____   #_____Name_____

                                        Date_____

Homework: True Stories

<u>Part I:</u>
Karen, a friend of mine who has twin girls, wrote me this e-mail message:
Yesterday I bought the girls new shoes, and I stopped to get new shoelaces
because the ones that come with the shoes are never long enough. I
couldn't decide between 24 inches and 27 inches, so I took the lace out of
one shoe so I could measure it. I folded the lace in half, so I could see if it
looked like 12 inches. The guy at the checkout counter said <u>"Oh that one
you have is 24 inches for sure because if it was 27 inches it wouldn't be
even - you know the ends wouldn't match up because 27 isn't an even
number."</u>

  1. Reread the story, and get a string or shoelace and think about it. Do
     you agree or disagree with the checkout guy's statement? Explain
     your reasoning with words, numbers, and well-labeled pictures.
  2. Would you have said anything to the checkout guy? Why or why not?
     If yes, how would you have responded?

Over!

FIGURE 1.5B   *Cathy Fossum's True Stories Homework (cont'd)*

3. Mr. Spicer ate 1/2 pizza. Ms. Fossum ate 1/2 pizza. Ms. Fossum said
she ate more pizza than Mr. Spicer. Could she be right?   Explain your
reasoning with words, numbers, and labeled diagrams.

Part II.
Complete 6 of the following 8 problems for credit, all 8 if you can. <u>Show</u>
your work, so I can see how you solved them. If you use lined paper, staple
it on. **Please no adult help**. Reason them out by yourself. Doublecheck
your answers. You can get help in the morning if needed.

1. 91-36 = _____   2. 7 X 48 =_____

3. $1.65 X 6 =_____   4. 10 X 135 = _____

5. 700 - 199 = _____   6. 295 X 8 = _____

7. 1000 ÷ 50 = _____   8. 800 ÷ 25 = _____

FIGURE 1.6 *Cathy Fossum's Agree or Disagree Homework*

#_____Name_____

Date_____

Homework: Agree or Disagree

Complete at least 4 of the 5 for credit, <u>all 5 if you can</u>.
Staple your paper to this sheet.   Explain your thinking
using words, numbers, and if it helps, pictures.

Student   Teacher

_____ _____ I have explained my thinking clearly and <u>completely</u>.

_____ _____ My ideas make sense.

_____ _____ I have completed at least 4 of the 5.

_____ _____ I have reread and edited my work.

_____ _____ ***I HAVE REMEMBERED TO BRING AT LEAST 1 BOX WITH A TOP TO SCHOOL. (THE TOP CAN BE ATTACHED OR SEPARATE.)***

1. Mr. Noriega set up 20 rows of chairs with 25 chairs in each. He asked Khou If he would have enough chairs to seat all the 652 students at Fremont School. She said, "I could skip count to find out how many chairs there are. Then I could answer your question." Do you agree or disagree? Explain why you think so.

2. Hexagons are 6-sided shapes that should have sides of equal length. Do you agree or disagree? Explain why you think so.

3. A 400 yard running track is longer than 1000 feet. Do you agree or disagree? Explain why you think so.

4. I wanted to ship oranges to my father for Christmas. Each of my boxes holds 16 oranges. To ship 165 oranges, I will need 10 boxes. Do you agree or disagree? Explain why you think so.

5. To multiply 156 x 4 you can do these simpler problems and add them together:

$$100 \times 4$$
$$5 \times 4$$
$$6 \times 4$$

Do you agree or disagree? Explain why you think so.

If 3 Is 5% of a Number, What Is 30% of That Number?

This assignment, at first glance, doesn't seem very difficult: it's only one problem. But when I asked my sixth graders to solve this problem for homework, I also asked them to take notes about how they solved it. They knew we were going to discuss how they thought as well as what answer they got. The assignment meant I was as interested in their thinking as I was in their answer.

It's human nature to expect that others will have solved a problem the same way you did; I am always surprised at the flexibility and the ingenuity of my students. The class period in which we all shared our approaches of thinking about this problem convinced me that the rote teaching of the three methods of solving percent problems is far less satisfactory than developing students' wider, overarching sense of number.

Deema said, "I found out that one percent of the number is three divided by five, since three is five percent." She paused to make sure that the class and I were understanding her thinking. (I jokingly call Deema the one-percent queen, because her preferred method of solving anything to do with percents is to find out what one percent of something is and use that information to arrive at the answer she is seeking.) "The answer is three fifths, which I know is point six." Deema has an unusual facility with the relationship between decimals and fractions. Although this facility is a teacher's dream, it sometimes causes problems for her with her peers, who are intimidated by her obvious affection for numbers and their relationships. "Since I want thirty percent, I just multiply point six by thirty, and I get eighteen. The answer is eighteen."

I wrote what she said in shorthand on the board: *Find 1% and then × by 30.*

"I did the same thing," said Lisa, "but you didn't call on me first."

Although I suspected that Lisa probably solved the problem in a different way, I noted her satisfaction when I put her name under Deema's and put an arrow going up to Deema's method. And I was indeed grateful that another student had aligned herself with Deema's way of thinking.

Joan, who can be impulsive, said, "I didn't do that at all. I knew that there were six fives in thirty, so there must be six threes in the number. That number is eighteen."

I wrote: *5 × 6 = 30 so 3 × 6 = the number we're looking for.*

Simone looked chagrined. "I guess what I did wasn't very efficient, but I learned how to set up ratios for everything, and that's what I am comfortable with. I made two ratios. The first was to find the whole number. I wrote three over *n* equals five over one hundred. Then I cross-multiplied, and I knew that five *n* is the same as three hundred, so the whole number is sixty. Then I wrote *n* over sixty is the same as thirty over one hundred to see what thirty percent of the whole number would be. I got eighteen also." She shrugged. "I couldn't think of any other way to get it."

Charlotte said, "You know how you call Deema the one-percent queen? Well, I must be the ten-percent queen. If three is five percent of a number then six must be ten percent of the number and if six is ten percent, then three times six, or eighteen, is thirty percent of the number."

"Wow, that makes so much sense!" said John, amazed by Charlotte's simple explanation. Charlotte was not a very confident math student, and this was the first year she had been engaged by these ideas. I was pleased that John had recognized her contribution so positively. And I, too, appreciated the elegant simplicity of her method.

"So, John," I asked, "how did you solve this problem?"

"I solved it wrong," he said.

"How did you start to think about it?"

"Well, my dad always says to draw a picture, and that's a good idea, but I don't always know what picture to draw."

"Let's see if we can help," I suggested. I drew a big rectangle and divided it into ten long thin rectangles. "Each of these is ten percent," I offered.

Sam chimed in, "Just cut them in half, and then each will be five percent."

I colored one twentieth in and labeled it *five percent.*

John got excited. "I know, you count by fives and color one of those sections in each time until you get to thirty. Let's see, you'd color in six of them. That's sixty percent."

"No," said Mike, correcting John, "I thought about it that way too, but without the picture. I said that five percent is one twentieth and twenty times three is sixty, so that means sixty is the whole number. Finding thirty percent of sixty is eighteen."

"Wait," said John. "What does that have to do with my picture? I didn't have to figure out the whole number, I just know that I colored in six blocks and each one is worth three. Oh yeah, that means eighteen is thirty percent. I agree with Mike."

Alex offered this explanation (Alex is dreamy, imaginative, and very creative and enthusiastic; I'm sure he'll be a writer someday): "I pretended that five percent is fifty percent. So if three was fifty percent and not five percent, then six would be the whole number because three is fifty percent of six. See?" I paused in my shorthand, trying to follow his reasoning. "Then, if six were the whole number and you took thirty percent of it, you'd multiply by three tenths and get one and eight tenths. But I made it fifty percent instead of five percent, so now I have to multiply my answer by ten!"

I wasn't sure whether anyone else had followed Alex's reasoning, which was more convoluted than anything anyone else had volunteered. But I appreciated his ability to know that if you multiply two things and you divided one of them by ten, you can multiply the other by ten and get the same answer. (At least I think what he did was based on this principle!)

David and Russell said they agreed with Joan. "And," Russell added, "even if we didn't do it that way, we think that makes the most sense to us now."

Andrew had worked with two equivalent fractions. "I wrote five divided by three, because five percent of the number is three, and I made that equal to thirty divided by n, since thirty percent is going to be the number we are looking for."

Rebecca said she agreed with Andrew's method.

We had been working all year on explaining what numbers mean when we write them. It is a difficult task, and I was very pleased with how far the students had come. At the end of the class I said, "One of the things I like best in this class is the way you really listen to one another and are able to say that your idea is just like someone else's. And if it's a little different, you make the connection. It means you are listening carefully and comparing your thinking to the thinking of others in class."

I used to worry about spending so much class time discussing a homework assignment. After all, there is so much curriculum to cover. However, an analysis of the results presented in the *Third International Math and Science Study* (1996–98) suggests that we are covering too many things in too little depth. What we really want is thorough understanding as opposed to an acquaintance with a wide variety of topics. Of course I feel pressured to prepare kids for the following year, but I feel even more pressured to make sure they understand the mathematics they are learning this year.

Ten years ago I would never have spent nearly one whole period discussing one problem. Back then my own mathematics was not secure enough to follow the reasoning of children who did not think about a problem the same way I did (Alex's explanation would have sent me over the edge). Nor did I understand that children need to learn many ways to think about a problem: my job was to give each child one surefire way (usually the traditional algorithm) to solve problems efficiently. Now I want my students not only to develop their own strategies but also to examine the thinking of others in case some other way of approaching a problem makes more sense.

Assigning homework surely means choosing problems that will enhance understanding. But it also means figuring out which homework assignments just get passed in and which will become rich opportunities for in-depth conversation, which homework assignments will be springboards for the day's lesson, and which will go from home directly into the grade book.

Additional Homework Assignments That Promote Practice

Number Jumble

SOURCE: adapted from *Developing Math Processes*
EMPHASIS: *place value, number sense*

You can use this assignment to cement children's understanding of the relationship between a digit and its value as determined by its place in a number. The assignment also forces children to think about how zeroes behave differently from counting numbers.

1. Using each digit only once, write the largest four-digit number possible with the digits 1, 3, 4, and 7.

2. Using each digit only once, write the smallest four-digit number possible with the digits 1, 3, 4, and 7.

3. What is the largest four-digit number you can write?

4. What is the smallest four-digit number you can write?

5. What is the largest four-digit number you can write using four different digits?

6. What is the smallest four-digit number you can write using four different digits?

7. Write four three-digit numbers in which the hundreds digit is half of the ones digit.

8. Write three four-digit numbers in which the thousands digit is double the tens digit.

9. Can you write a four-digit number whose digits add up to 36? 37? 34?

10. Can you write a four-digit number whose digits add up to 8?

11. Using four different digits, can you write a number whose digits add up to 6?

What Three-Digit Number Could I Be?

SOURCE: adapted from *Developing Math Processes*
EMPHASIS: *number sense, logical reasoning*

This assignment develops children's understanding of three-digit numbers. Some of the questions have only one answer and some have many. I like to let my students test their guesses using number tiles and blank one-inch squares.

1. My three digits add up to 8. What number could I be?

2. Each of my three digits is the same, and they add up to 21. What number could I be?

3. Each of my three digits is even, each one is a different number, and their sum is between 10 and 19. What number could I be?

4. My three digits add up to 11. What number could I be?

5. Two of my three digits are odd, the remaining one is even, and their sum is less than 10. What number could I be?

6. Each of my three digits is odd, my tens digit is larger than my hundreds digit, and the sum of my three digits is less than 9. What number could I be?

Shoot the Outlaw

EMPHASIS: *practicing facts, finding patterns*

Students usually love problems that involve deciding which number in a group of numbers does not belong. Be sure you listen carefully to children's reasoning. There are many ways to think about numbers, and good mathematical thinkers can justify almost any choice they make!

Shoot the outlaw in this group of numbers:

| 3, | 12, | 10, | 7 |

Possible solutions:

The outlaw is 12, because you can make an addition or subtraction fact using the other numbers: 3 plus 7 is 10, and 10 minus 7 is 3.

The outlaw is 7 because it is the only number that does not begin with *t* when written as a word.

Shoot the outlaw in this group of numbers:

| 134, | 449, | 346, | 278, | 522, | 380 |

Possible solutions:

The outlaw is 449, because it is odd.

The outlaw is 522, because it is the only number in which the digit in the tens place is smaller than the digit in the hundreds place.

———————

Shoot the outlaw in this group of numbers:

| 9 | 14 | 5 | 3 |

Possible solutions:

The outlaw is 3, because 9 and 5 equal 14.

The outlaw is 14, because it is the only two-digit number.

The outlaw is 14, because it is the only even number.

The outlaw is 14, because it is the only number that does not end in the letter e when written as a word.

The outlaw is 9, because it is the only square number.

———————

Shoot the outlaw in this group of numbers:

| 7 | 5 | 8 | 12 |

Possible solutions:

The outlaw is 8, because 7 and 5 equals 12.

The outlaw is 8, because it is the only cubed number ($2 \times 2 \times 2$).

The outlaw is 8, because it doesn't have the letter *v* in it when it is written as a word.

The outlaw is 12, because it has two digits.

———————

Shoot the outlaw in this group of numbers:

| 2 | 6 | 5 | 10 |

Possible solutions:

The outlaw is 2, because it is the only number that when rounded to the nearest ten, would not equal 10.

The outlaw is 5, because it is the only odd number.

The outlaw is 10, because it is the only two-digit number.

The outlaw is 6, because it is the only number that is not a factor of 10.

EMPHASIS: *computation, number sense*

Plus or Minus

$$\begin{array}{cc} \square\ \square & \square\ \square \\ -\ \square & +\ \square \end{array}$$

Using only the digits 3, 5, and 7 and an addition or subtraction sign, is it possible to combine a two-digit and one-digit number to produce the following sums or differences: 72? 60? 32? 78? 28? 46? 68? 54? 42? (For example: 75 – 3 = 72.)

EMPHASIS: *number sense, arithmetic*

Operation Zero

This is a game for two players. Player A chooses any three-digit number less than or equal to 900 and punches it into a calculator. Player B must reduce this initial number to zero in at most five calculations, using any of the four basic operations of arithmetic and a single-digit number (not zero) each time. Players record each operation and the result as they go along.

Example:

Player A chooses 965 as the number. Player B

- divides by 5 to get 193 (calculation 1)

- subtracts 4 to get 189 (calculation 2)

- divides by 9 to get 21 (calculation 3)

- divides by 7 to get 3 (calculation 4), and

- subtracts 3 to get 0 (calculation 5).

EMPHASIS: *area and perimeter*
NOTE: Allow more than one night for this assignment, and don't assume that every student will have access to a newspaper at home. Have some old ones available in class for those who need them.

Newspaper Geometry

Cut out five photos from a newspaper. What is the perimeter of each (in centimeters)? What is the area of each? Arrange them in order, beginning with the one with the smallest area.

EMPHASIS: *identifying and comparing fractions*

Vowel Fractions

Choose ten words that contain various numbers of letters. They can be names of friends, randomly selected words, your weekly vocabulary list, whatever. Figure out what fraction of the letters in each word are vowels. Arrange the words in order from those that have the smallest fraction of vowels to those that have the largest. Be prepared to explain how you compared and to contribute your words to a class chart.

Company for Dinner

EMPHASIS: *fractions, ratio and proportion*

NOTE: You may also choose a recipe and give each student a copy.

Choose a recipe from a cookbook and adjust the amounts of the ingredients so that you will be able to feed everyone in the class.

Math
Homework
as
Preparation

Another approach to homework is as a way to gather data that will be useful to the student or the class during an upcoming lesson. Instead of submitting their completed homework to you, the students share their work and ideas with one another. This approach makes it immediately obvious who has and hasn't done the assignment, and that subtle pressure energizes some reluctant students. Those who have completed the homework have a personal context and a foundation for understanding.

Students in the primary grades can complete easy surveys: the number of people that live in their house, how many forks will be on their table when it is set for Thanksgiving dinner, the number of doors or windows in their house, the number of shoes in their closet, how many pieces of mail arrive in their mailbox on a particular day or during a particular week. Intermediate-grade children can collect more sophisticated data: the average amount of their household's monthly electric bill, the number of words in a paragraph of a book they have read, the number of minutes they spend on homework on a particular day, the number and duration of long distance phone calls made from their home during the previous month, how many items their parents purchased during their most recent trip to the grocery store.

Example Activities

Multiplication Matrix

Here's the assignment: *How many different answers will you get if you multiply every single-digit number except zero by every other single-digit number except zero? Arrange these answers in order, from smallest to largest.*

There are lots of ways students can approach this problem. They can write out all the combinations. They can start with a list of possible answers and work backward to see whether they can construct a problem that has each answer. Or they can prepare some kind of chart or graph or table.

I gave this assignment to my fourth-grade class one day, then talked with them a bit to get them started. "In working this problem, you will be considering all the multiplication facts from one times one through nine times nine. In other words, you must multiply every possible combination of two one-digit numbers except zero. Remember, I'm not interested in how many problems you can make, but in how many *different answers* there are to these problems. And I don't want you to use a calculator, because if you do, I won't be able to tell what you were thinking as you worked. Besides practicing these computations is a good thing. So keep track of your work in writing, and tomorrow we'll talk about what you discovered. But first, how many answers do you think there will be? Take a guess before you start. What will the largest answer be? What will the smallest answer be?"

The next day we had a spirited discussion. There are 36 different answers in the one-digit multiplication tables, and many of the students had come up with this number or one close to it. It was very liberating for them to discover that there are only 36 possible answers in all of the multiplication tables they have to memorize! And it was very enlightening for me to discover the ways in which they had organized their thinking. Here's what individual students said they had done:

- I used a chart.

- I used patterns to help. For example, I knew that two times two equals four, so each time I raised the number I was multiplying by one (two times three, two times four, and so on) my answer went up by two.

- I did it the hard way: I wrote down all the equations in the times tables and crossed out duplicate answers.

- I used what I knew about reverses. After I'd done three times six, I didn't have to do six times three. If my first number was larger than the number I was multiplying by, I'd already gotten that answer.

- I started over after I saw a pattern developing.

- I asked my parents whether I needed to write all the problems or just some of them.

- I tried to be efficient: after I did the one times table, I started the two times table with two times five, because all the numbers up through nine had already appeared.

■ I used a backward strategy: I started with the nine times table and worked down.

■ I used an old multiplication chart and made a new chart of how many numbers between 1 and 81 appeared no times, one time, two times, three times, or four times (the most often).

■ I filled in only half of a chart, since the mirror reverse was already accounted for.

■ I started with the answers from 1 to 81 and then tried to find problems to match.

■ I looked at how many numbers between 1 and 81 *are* the answers to one-digit multiplication problems (36) compared with how many *are not* (45) and wondered whether there was any significance to the difference of 9.

Building on this first assignment, I then gave the class a related homework activity, multiplication tic-tac-toe (see figure 2.1), a game that uses the 36 answers to one-digit multiplication problems they had been exploring. I asked each student to play the game with someone at home during the following week and return the completed game sheet.

This game gives students lots of practice with multiplication and encourages them to develop strategies for producing the products they need to win and for preventing their opponent from producing the products she or he needs to win. It generates a real interest in knowing which products have more than one pair of factors.

For older children, you can give a nearly identical assignment using the decimals .1 through .9. Answers on the grid will be between .01 and .81. I have also experimented with having students figure out all the possible sums of the fractions $\frac{1}{2}$, $\frac{1}{4}$, $\frac{1}{3}$, $\frac{2}{3}$, $\frac{1}{6}$, $\frac{1}{8}$, $\frac{3}{8}$, $\frac{3}{4}$, and $\frac{5}{8}$. (I got 24 different answers, so I included the number 1 twice in a five-by-five grid.)

FIGURE 2.1 *Multiplication Tic-Tac-Toe*

Multiplication Tic-Tac-Toe

This game for two people requires two small markers, such as paper clips or pennies. The first player puts the two markers in the row of digits appearing below the grid, either on two different digits or on the same digit (being able to put them on the same digit allows you to multiply a digit by itself). He or she multiplies the two numbers identified by the markers together, produces a product, and places an X over that product on the game board. The second player moves ONE of the markers to a different digit, produces a product from the numbers so identified, and draws a circle around this new product on the game board. Play alternates in this way, each player moving only one marker at a time to a different digit, until one player has captured four squares in a row (horizontally, vertically, or diagonally).

1	2	3	4	5	6
7	8	9	10	12	14
15	16	18	20	21	24
25	27	28	30	32	35
36	40	42	45	48	49
54	56	63	64	72	81

1 2 3 4 5 6 7 8 9

The lovesick giver of very eccentric gifts in the song "The Twelve Days of Christmas" had to do a great deal of shopping to impress the object of his or her affection. If you'll remember, the gifts included:

The Twelve Days of Christmas

> a partridge in a pear tree
> two turtle doves
> three French hens
> four calling birds
> five gold rings
> six geese a-laying
> seven swans a-swimming
> eight maids a-milking
> nine ladies dancing
> ten lords a-leaping
> eleven pipers piping
> twelve drummers drumming

You may also remember that the gift giving was cumulative. That is, on each day, the loved one received the gift for that day, in the appropriate quantity, as well as duplicates of all the gifts received up to that point.

These gifts can be the basis of a very complex sums-of-series math problem that involves patterns galore and that can be solved in many different ways. I introduced the problem in class, presenting it to two classes of fourth graders like this:

> The poor lovesick person who is arranging for gifts for the twelve days of Christmas is having a difficult time getting organized and has asked our math class to help out. Basically you have two jobs:
>
> 1. Figure out the total number of presents that will need to be purchased in order to send all the things mentioned in the song. See if you can find a system and patterns to help you. Record your work, and be able to explain how you arrived at your answer. There are lots of neat ways to approach this problem. Have fun!
>
> 2. Figure out how many of each kind of gift will need to be ordered. For example, you would order twelve partridges and twelve pear trees, one for each of the twelve days! (Would they be cheaper by the dozen? Hmm! But for now we aren't concerned with the cost.)

The students set to work in small groups, and each group seemed to approach the problem differently.

One group found out how many gifts arrived on the first day, how many on the second, how many on the third, and so on (see figure 2.2). They identified a pattern, and one very precocious student recognized the triangular numbers (1 gift on day one, 3 additional gifts on day two, 6 additional gifts on day three, and so on). With a calculator, they added the total number of each day's presents.

Another group noticed that twelve partridges in pear trees were sent (one for all twelve days), twenty-two turtle doves (two on each of eleven days), and so on (see figure 2.3). They added these numbers up. If you use this approach,

FIGURE 2.2   *How Many Gifts on Each Day*

Dear Mrs. Raphel,
I think the answer is 364. Now let's take a look at my chart, shall we? On day one, I would have received 1 present, a partridge in a pear tree. On the second day, I would have gotten 3 presents, two turtle doves (2), and a partridge in a pear tree (3). But, we forgot about the first present, so that means I'd have to add the total up, so I did it at the end. Now, I'm pleased to see you've chosen my answer. Very nice choice.

Day	Presents
1	1
2	3
3	6
4	10
5	15
6	21
7	28
8	36
9	45
10	55
11	66
12	78
	364

FIGURE 2.3   *How Many of Each Gift*

Dear Mrs. Raphel,

This is how I got my answer of 364:

1. Partridge x 12 days = 12

2. Turtle Doves x 11 days = 22

3. French Hens x 10 days = 30

4. Calling Birds x 9 days = 36

5. Golden Rings x 8 days = 40

6. Geese x 7 days = 42

7. Swans x 6 days = 42

8. Maids x 5 days = 40

9. Ladies x 4 days = 36

10. Lords x 3 days = 30

11. Pipers x 2 days = 22

12. Drummers x 1 days = 12

                          3 6 4

as they did, you will notice the same remarkable pattern emerging that they did. The excitement of discovering that the number of six egg-laying geese sent for seven days is the same as the number of seven swimming swans sent for six days heightened when the students realized that the pattern held true in other configurations (for example, the number of five gold rings sent for eight days is the same as the number of eight milking maids sent for five days). Never had I seen the commutative property of multiplication generate so many simultaneous ah-has!

Still another group started with the last day, discovering that they had to add 1 + 2 + 3 + 4 + 5 + 6 + 7 + 8 + 9 + 10 + 11 + 12 (sums-of-series!) to get 78 total gifts. Working backward, they saw that on the next to last day they had to add the same string of numbers except for the 12.

One group began by adding 12 (the drummers drumming) to 11 and 11 (the pipers piping on days 11 and 12), to 10 and 10 and 10 (the leaping lords on days 10, 11, and 12), and so on. Their final list of operations looked like this: 12 + 11 + 11 + 10 + 10 + 10 + 9 + 9 + 9 + 9 + 8 + 8 + 8 + 8 + 8 + 7 + 7 + 7 + 7 + 7 + 7 + 6 + 6 + 6 + 6 + 6 + 6 + 6 + 5 + 5 + 5 + 5 + 5 + 5 + 5 + 5 + 4 + 4 + 4 + 4 + 4 + 4 + 4 + 4 + 4 + 3 + 3 + 3 + 3 + 3 + 3 + 3 + 3 + 3 + 3 + 2 + 2 + 2 + 2 + 2 + 2 + 2 + 2 + 2 + 2 + 1 + 1 + 1 + 1 + 1 + 1 + 1 + 1 + 1 + 1 + 1. Then they linked all numbers equaling 10. That is, they added the four 9s to four of the ones, the five 8s to five of the 2s, the six 7s to six of the 3s, and the seven 6s to seven of the 4s. Finally they combined the eight 5s into four 10s and bunched the remaining unused numbers into groups of 10 as well.

All the groups, regardless of their method, arrived at the staggering and unexpected total of 364 gifts that had to be ordered. They also all figured out, some more elegantly than others, that the ordering form had to look something like this:

> 12 partridges in pear trees
> 22 turtle doves
> 30 French hens
> 36 calling birds
> 40 gold rings
> 42 geese a-laying
> 42 swans a-swimming
> 40 maids a-milking
> 36 ladies dancing
> 30 lords a-leaping
> 22 pipers piping
> 12 drummers drumming

Seeing the wonderful patterns, the diminishing intervals between numbers, and the symmetry of this numerical list, the children were fascinated and energized. They eagerly shared their methods of arriving at the answer, identifying the moment when they stopped dealing with the raw data and let the emerging pattern do the work for them.

I now told the students that the gift giver also wanted us to figure out approximately what it would cost to send all these things. As homework, I asked each child to research the cost of one of the twelve categories of presents (they could choose the category, and pairs or teams of students could work together, but I made sure each type of gift was being investigated). I gave them a full week in which to complete their investigation and told them they could contact any people or organizations they needed to. Here's the assignment I gave them:

> Let's help this person figure out approximately how much money it will cost to send all these gifts. We'll work on this as a whole class. We'll divide up the presents, and each person or team will have only one to research. You may have to make some telephone calls and speak to people. For example, how much would it cost to hire eleven musicians to be the pipers piping? How many days would you need them for? The person investigating this could call the New England Conservatory, the Boston Symphony Orchestra, or one of those folks who advertise that they will play at your party. Or you may find a small statue of a flute player at the mall and decide to send eleven of those instead—the form of the gift is your decision Whenever you ask someone for help or information, remember to be polite and explain the project you are working on. Attach all your documentation to this sheet, and have fun! Be prepared to report back to class next week.

The data and the stories that came back a week later were a real pleasure to read and hear! Because this was a group project and the class, as a community, was depending on the information, no child was unprepared, although some had invested more energy and creativity than others had. However, each child was eager to share his or her experiences, and for the most part (there were a few exceptions) everyone reported receiving positive responses when they explained this math assignment to the outside world. Some children worked together, some did the research by phone, some did it in person. Parents, baby-sitters, older siblings, and community merchants were all called upon for advice and information. Many students first had to deal with problems of interpretation. Would they hire actors to be the lords a-leaping, and if so, for how long? Would they have to include transportation costs? What is a partridge, anyway? If you can't find one, what would be a good substitute?

While the anecdotes generated by this investigation will not advance your mathematical understanding, some are so irresistible they deserve to be shared. Terrence called the Boston Recreation Department to find out how much the swan boats in the Boston Public Gardens cost to rent and was told what a popular singing group had been charged when they used the boats in a music video. Justin couldn't find out anything about live geese but went to a butcher shop and found out the price per pound for goose and the average weight of the geese that were available. This led him into calculations with fractions and decimals! Beth used a tree catalogue to find out the cost of a pear tree. Diana asked a high school teacher known for playing the bagpipes during special occasions how much it would cost to rent him. Amelia added the money for cages and bird seed to the price of her partridges; she wanted them to be comfortable and stay alive. Kiran had to tell the maid service she called how many rooms her house had and how many times a month she was considering using the service, as well as assure the service that the house was in the appropriate regional district. Tatiana, who was in rehearsal at the time for a production of *The Nutcracker* with the Boston Ballet, talked with the ballerinas about how much the dancing ladies might expect to be paid.

We consolidated the information we had collected by filling out a chart with the following headings: *Researcher, Type of Gift, Source of Price, Price for One, Number Needed, Total.* Two classes were involved in this project, so we ended up with two sets of independently researched data. (One group also wanted to figure out the Massachusetts sales tax of five percent, which led to a rich if somewhat off-the-track conversation about computing it.) The children were interested in their own information, but were also curious about how their prices compared with those the other class had turned up. Here are the totals:

Class 1		Class 2	
12 partridges (cockatiels)	720.00	12 partridges	186.00
12 pear trees	360.00	12 pear trees	167.00
22 turtle doves	660.00	22 turtle doves	595.00
30 French hens	269.91	30 French hens	297.00
36 calling birds	108,000.00	36 calling birds (parrots)	108,000.00
40 gold rings	33,460.00	40 gold rings	2,200.00
42 geese	966.00	42 geese	1,239.00
42 swans	840.00	42 swans	1,050.00
40 maids	3,620.00	40 maids	2,000.00
40 cows	2,000.00	40 cows for milking	36,000.00
36 ladies dancing	360.00	36 ladies dancing	9,671.60
30 lords a-leaping	1,500.00	30 lords a-leaping	3,000.00
22 pipers piping	7,921.92	22 pipers piping	2,168.96
12 drummers drumming	1,680.00	12 drummers	480.00
Grand Total	162,357.83	Grand Total	167,054.96

Were the totals far apart? The students agreed that $5,000 is a lot of money, generally, but in relation to the two big amounts, it was pretty close. What accounted for the discrepancies? Was it interpretation or computation? What was the average of the two figures? (Some students figured this out using a calculator, but others performed inverse operations on both numbers until they were the same. That is, whatever amount they added to the smaller number, they subtracted from the larger number. They started with $2,000 and worked their way to the middle using ever smaller amounts, eventually coming up with $164,706.34 (rounded off to the nearest hundredth, since the difference between the two numbers was odd). Figuring the sales tax and the average were not questions on a worksheet. They were not part of a lesson. The children were taking the data they had created and struggling to make sense of the information.

Although we weren't able to share the results of this project during a school assembly or a parents night, we really needed an audience. Great discoveries assume a larger importance only if they are shared, and we were determined to capture the mathematical power of what we had done and display what we had learned. The students transcribed the results of their research onto pieces of poster board, added illustrations, and hung their work outside the auditorium at the winter concert. Much to our surprise and pleasure, the local newspaper did a story on this same problem a week later.

Some of you are probably thinking that the children in your class could never handle this assignment and that their parents couldn't or wouldn't provide the necessary support. The objections spring immediately to mind: the project doesn't look enough like math, it will take too much time, it's too complicated, students don't generally do well with long-range projects. And I certainly don't expect you to adopt all the ideas in this book verbatim. You have to decide what makes sense in your classroom and in your community. One teacher I know substituted other, more relevant presents (CD players, Nintendo games, bicycles) and provided catalogues and sale circulars for students to use to determine prices. Another teacher, who was uncomfortable with the Christmas theme, did a similar project for the "thirteen days of Halloween," with the gift giver bestowing different kinds of candy (Maryann Wickett's article in the bibliography is an inspiring account of this assignment).

It turns out that our school's fourth graders have not been alone in their enchantment with the mathematical ramifications of this song. In Irene Trivas's marvelous picture book *Emma's Christmas*, Emma receives the aforementioned presents from a prince (what happens at the end of the tale is simply a delight). Similar tales, minus the Christmas context, include Seymour Chwast's *The Twelve Circus Rings* and Elizabeth Lee O'Donnell's *The Twelve Days of Summer*.

An assignment like this is a terrific inducement to higher-order thinking. Lauren Resnick, in *Education and Learning to Think* (1987), posits nine criteria for identifying higher-order thinking, so let's look at the assignment specifically in those terms:

1. *Higher-order thinking is nonalgorithmic.* The path of action is not fully specified in advance. These fourth graders were given an intriguing problem, along with a great deal of latitude in how to solve it. Although the initial investigation of the total number of presents has one correct answer, there are many ways to get that answer. And the independent research into pricing is left largely up to the student. Deciding where and to whom to go for information and what to do if the information doesn't align exactly with what you need to know involves flexible thinking and repeated reassessments of whether you are accomplishing your goal.

2. *Higher-order thinking tends to be complex.* The total path is not visible from any single vantage. For this problem, parts of the strategy are clear: once you find a per-unit price for something and know how many of these gifts you need to order, you multiply; then you add to get a grand total. But there is no one way to verify the data, because the information required is out of the ordinary and subject to interpretation.

3. *Higher-order thinking often yields multiple solutions, each with costs and benefits, rather than unique solutions.* The data generated by the two classes make it clear that there is no one right answer to this problem. Children have to decide how to find the information (where to go, with whom to talk, whether to use the telephone or go in person, whether to work alone or with a partner), but they also need to evaluate what they find out. Is this a really generous person who will choose the top of the line in every category, or is he or she perhaps attempting to disguise a lack of quality with quantity?

4. *Higher-order thinking involves nuance and judgment.* What if the maids say they will do windows but not milk cows? (True story.) What is a calling bird, exactly? What if partridges are out of season? Are boats in the shape of swans more or less appropriate than little swan charms that dangle from a bracelet?

5. *Higher-order thinking involves the application of conflicting criteria.* Piping pipers might have been common when the song was written but are fairly hard to identify and order these days. Is it okay to send frozen geese suitable for a sumptuous meal, even though the words of the song clearly imply the geese are alive?

6. *Higher-order thinking often involves uncertainty.* Not everything that bears on the task is known. Are you paying with cash, check, or credit card? Do you include cages and feed when sending partridges? Do the dancers get paid by the hour? Do they charge transportation? Do you pay tax on both goods and services?

7. *Higher-order thinking involves self-regulation.* Listening to children talk about their initial ideas, why they rejected them, where they went for help, and what kind of help they sought made it clear that many of these children were as aware of their strategies as they were of the mathematical problem they were interpreting. They spoke as fourth graders, with a rare eloquence, of how they knew they were going down dead ends, of the limitations of their solutions (it does say geese a-laying, and the ones in the butcher shop can hardly be expected to do that, sigh), what they would have liked to do given unlimited time, resources, and courage. The problem was constructed loosely enough so that the children not only had to solve it, they had to shape it first.

8. *Higher-order thinking involves imposing meaning, finding structure in apparent disorder.* When the maids said that they would do a house but not milk a cow, a very young and patient voice explained that they would not actually be doing this, but if they were, what would be the charge. In fact, probably the only people who really had an easy time of the whole project were those who found out the cost of gold rings. But even they discussed whether you went with the top of the line, or whether you shopped on sale (honest). One astute fourth grader said that if the maiden was getting just one ring, he would have bought the most expensive, but the quantity that was being ordered precluded going for quality.

9. *Higher-order thinking is effortful.* There is considerable mental work involved in the kinds of elaboration and judgments required.

Additional Homework Assignments Geared Toward Preparation

EMPHASIS: *organizing information, identifying patterns*

Ways to Make Change for a Quarter

Letting kids know that there are more than ten ways will help them persevere. You might ask: How will you know when you have found them all? Is there a system for making sure you have included all of them? Questions for class discussion include: Do any of the combinations use the same number of coins? Which combination uses the fewest coins? the most? Super challenge: How many ways can you make change for a dollar without using pennies?

EMPHASIS: *divisibility, patterns*

Remainder Riddles

SOURCE: based on *A Remainder of One*, by Elinor Pinczes, as discussed by Rusty Bresser in *Math and Literature, Grades 4–6*

Here are the riddles:

My number is between 1 and 25
When you divide my number by 1, the remainder is 0
When you divide my number by 2, the remainder is 1
When you divide my number by 3, the remainder is 1
When you divide my number by 4, the remainder is 3
When you divide my number by 5, the remainder is 4
When you divide my number by 6, the remainder is 1
When you divide my number by 7, the remainder is 5

My number is between 1 and 100
When you divide my number by 1, the remainder is 0
When you divide my number by 2, the remainder is 0
When you divide my number by 3, the remainder is 1
When you divide my number by 4, the remainder is 2
When you divide my number by 5, the remainder is 4
When you divide my number by 6, the remainder is 4
When you divide my number by 7, the remainder is 3

Here are some strategies my students have used to solve these riddles:

- Start with the last clue. There are fewer numbers divisible by seven than any other number.

- Find out if the number is odd or even, that way you eliminate half of the possibilities.

- Look at the clue about being divisible by five, because it tells you what the number will end in. For example, if the number is divisible by five and has a remainder of three, it has to end in a three or eight; you'll know which if you find out whether it is odd or even.

■ Numbers that have a remainder of zero when you divide them by three have to add up to a multiple of three.

■ Just try a number and do guess-and-check until you get it.

■ Color code by patterns.

Here's the homework assignment:

> I love riddles, and I especially love riddles with numbers in them. Because we read *A Remainder of One* today, I hope we also have new sensitivity for remainders. I had a lot of fun writing these remainder riddles for you to solve for homework. You have one week to solve them.
>
> In working with division facts, you are beginning to learn something about what mathematicians call *divisibility*. That means, with a little practice and some inside information, you can tell just by looking at a number or with just a little work, whether a number will have a remainder of zero when it is divided by a one-digit divisor. See whether you can discover some of those patterns. If you notice anything interesting (like what happens to all even numbers when you divide them by 2), make sure to jot yourself a note so that you can share your discoveries. I love discoveries almost as much as riddles!
>
> I would also like you to write a remainder riddle of your own. If you would like yours to be between 1 and 25, that's fine. If you want to be really adventurous, you may try one between 1 and 100. Please write your riddle very neatly so that you can pass it around for others in class to try. Have fun!
>
> P.S.: I wonder which number between 1 and 100 can be divided evenly (that is, with a remainder of 0) by the most one-digit numbers? This might be a fun investigation for you to attempt with your family.

For older children you might phrase an assignment this way: I am thinking of a number that has no remainder if you divide it by 1 or 3, has a remainder of 1 when divided by 2, and has a remainder of 3 when divided by 4, 6, or 7. What is its remainder if you divide it by 5?

Another interesting investigation for intermediate-grade children is: what are the fewest clues you can give and have only one number between one and a hundred be the answer? The new *Family Math* book for middle schoolers (Thompson and Mayfield-Ingram 1998, page 121) has a similar activity called Numerous Remainders that gives only two or three clues for a number. Here is an example: *Find a number that has a remainder of 6 when divided by 7 and a remainder of 3 when divided by 5.*

Can-It Fractions and Decimals

Using items in your pantry, can you come up with some fraction problems? Bring in the items and your question on a 5-by-8 file card. Please put the answer on the back. We'll work on some problems in class to get you started.

East Point Tiny Cleaned Shrimp, 4.25 oz.
Bumblebee Solid White Tuna in Water, $6\frac{1}{2}$ oz.

I want to be able to compare the weights of these two cans, but one is recorded in fractions and one in decimals. You'll need to start by converting the weights both to fractions or decimals.

     Weight of shrimp

     Weight of tuna

Which can looks bigger?

How much more does the heavier can weigh than the lighter one? Write how you got your answer.

Sun-Maid Raisins, $\frac{1}{2}$ oz.
Sun-Maid Golden Raisins, 15 oz.

How many of the little packages of raisins would you have to buy in order to get enough raisins to weigh the same amount as the big box?

Durkee Onion Gravy Mix, $\frac{3}{4}$ oz.
Good Seasons Italian Salad Dressing Mix, .7 oz

What fraction of an ounce does the onion gravy weigh?

What fraction of an ounce does the salad dressing weigh?

Which package weighs more? How much more?

When made according to directions, how much does each packet make?

Can you say that the more a packet weighs, the more it will make? Why or why not?

What is the price per pound of each of these products?

Dole Pineapple Slices, 20 oz. ($13\frac{1}{4}$ oz. pineapple)
Libby's Lite Fruit Cocktail, 16 oz. ($11\frac{3}{4}$ oz. fruit)

Which of these two cans contains more fruit? How much more?
Which of these two cans contains more liquid? How much more?
Can you tell which is a better buy? Share your thinking!

Durkee Onion Powder, $1\frac{1}{2}$ oz.
Durkee Onion Salt, $3\frac{3}{4}$ oz.

These two cost almost the same, but you get a lot more of the onion salt than the onion powder. Do you have a theory on why this might be so?
How much more onion salt is there than onion powder?
If you bought two new containers of onion powder, would it weigh as much as the onion salt you would get if you bought one new container of onion salt? How do you know?

Polaner All-Fruit Spreadable Fruit (Apricot), 15.25 oz.
Hero Strawberry Preserve, $1\frac{1}{2}$ oz.

How much more spreadable fruit is there than strawberry preserve?
About how many small jars of strawberry preserve would you have to buy to get as much product as you do in the jar of spreadable fruit? How do you know?

Kellogg's Special K, $\frac{9}{16}$ oz. individual serving
Wheaties, $\frac{3}{4}$ oz. individual serving

Compare these two cereals. Which one of these cereals weighs more? How much more? How do you know?

Libby's Cut Green Beans, 16 oz.

Cans of vegetables often have two weights, the net weight (which is what the whole can weighs, including the packing liquid) and the weight of the vegetables themselves.
How much of this can is water? Is more than half of this can vegetables? How do you know?

Mother's Rice Cakes, 4.5 oz.

This package contains 10 cakes, and each cake has 45 calories. If a piece of bread is approximately 60 calories, about how many pieces of bread would give you the same calorie count as this package of rice cakes?
This is a really hard problem. About how many ounces does each of the rice cakes weigh? Explain how you got your answer.

Orange Mint Tic Tacs, $\frac{1}{2}$ oz.
Russell Stover Mint Dreams, $1\frac{1}{8}$ oz.
Haribo Gold-Bears Gummi Candy, $1\frac{1}{2}$ oz.
Jolly Rancher Watermelon Candy, $1\frac{3}{4}$ oz.
Charleston Chew, $1\frac{7}{8}$ oz.
Russell Stover Marshmallow Nut Bar, $1\frac{1}{4}$ oz.

List these candies in order from the lightest to the heaviest. How did you get your answer? What strategies did you use?

Math
Homework
as
Extension

Homework can be at its most engaging when it asks students to extend what they have been taught and apply it to something new. An extension assignment gives them an opportunity to see how solid their foundation is and whether they can apply a class assignment, which has been structured for every student, in a way that is personally appropriate and appealing. Sometimes children discover they didn't understand what happened in class nearly as well as they thought they did.

Open-ended assignments like these are treasure troves for creative, motivated students, but can be pure terror for children who need structure in order to feel safe. Knowing your students allows you to provide scaffolding for those who need it and stay out of the way of those who don't.

In the intermediate grades it is a good idea to check in with students when they are working on long-term projects. They rarely have the discipline to manage time well. In addition, they need enough guidance so that they will be able to complete this kind of homework successfully. Nothing breeds success like success. One of a teacher's jobs is to figure out how to ensure that an assignment can be completed successfully. Not only will this further your own classroom agenda, but it is a gift to your colleagues who will teach these students in the years to come.

Example Activities

Finding Differences

With a fourth-grade class, I often use an activity from Robert Wirtz's *Banking on Problem Solving* (1976), in which we investigate how many different answers we can arrive at by making two-digit addends from the numbers 1, 3, 4, and 5—for example 35 + 41 = 76. While other combinations of these same digits will also produce the answer 76, the assignment is to produce different *answers*, not different problems. This challenge is perfect for the first few weeks of fourth grade because it involves no regrouping and yields many patterns that are both obvious and exciting to students. The focus on looking for patterns and making predictions provides a solid foundation.

Then, as a long-term homework assignment (they have a week in which to complete it), I give the students a different four-number grouping—2, 3, 5, and 9—this time asking them to see how many *answers* they can come up with by subtracting one two-digit number from another, both numbers being made from these four digits. This is a more difficult problem. For one thing, the magnitude of a number matters. Although some children have probably heard of negative numbers by this time, I specify that only positive differences are allowed; that is, the greater number has to be on top. The homework assignment is shown in figure 3.1.

This is not trivial homework. It expects children to use what they know about subtraction, although that knowledge may not be obvious to them. It asks them to come up with some kind of strategy for setting up the problems and for figuring out how any patterns they discover may make their work simple, elegant, and/or complete.

The first time I used this assignment, I was afraid it might be too complex so early in the year. I obsessed about whether my directions were clear enough. Would parents feel that this was too difficult, that they had to provide too much help? Or would they be intrigued by how rich the problem is? But I reasoned that any problem that prompts parents and children to talk about mathematics is a good problem.

Here are some of the things my students discovered:

1. I needed to be systematic when I did this problem.

2. There are only twelve answers.

3. Some answers have reverses; for example, 95 is possible and so is 59; 32 is possible and so is 23. The answers were always able to be reversed unless you regrouped. The only numbers that had reverses were two-digit answers where one digit is odd and one digit is even. There are four pairs of numbers where you could have the top number be the same and switch the bottom number so that you would get a reversal as an answer.

4. You could never have twenty-something on top, because it would be too small.

5. There are six different ways you can use a 9 in the tens place of the top number,

FIGURE 3.1   *Finding Differences*

How many different answers can you get when you subtract two two-digit numbers that contain only the digits 2, 3, 5, and 9? Remember, you need to use all four digits in each example, so you can't use the same digit more than once in each problem. Also, you can't produce any negative numbers this time, so the greater number always has to be on the top. Here's an example of one problem that you could make:

$$\begin{array}{r} 59 \\ -\ 23 \\ \hline 36 \end{array}$$

Before you start, guess how many different answers you think you can come up with. Don't be afraid to take a risk. Write your guess here:

Is there a way for you to organize your work so that you make sure you get all the possibilities? Make sure you work neatly so that you can read all your work easily. You might want to work on graph paper or the reverse side of this sheet.

After you have finished, think about whether you noticed anything interesting—any patterns, for example. Write at least one thing you noticed here:

four different ways you can use a 5 in the tens place of the top number, two different ways you can use a 3 in the tens place of the top number, and zero problems with a 2 in the tens place of the top number. It goes down by two each time.

6. None of the answers end in zero

7. There is one answer between 0–10, two answers between 10–20, two answers between 20–30, two answers between 30–40, one answer between 40–50, one answer between 50–60, two answers between 60–70, one answer between 70–80, and no answers between 80–90 or between 90–100. In any group of ten, there are never more than two answers. There are no answers with three digits in them. There is only one answer with one digit.

8. We can organize our work. One half of all the answers (six) are switches, and one half (six) are not.

9. When subtracting an odd number from another odd number, you always get an even number.

10. Here are the answers from least to greatest: 6, 13, 14, 24, 27, 36, 39, 41, 57, 63, 69, and 72.

11. If you list all the 23 digits that showed up in all the possible answers, this is what you get: 1, 1, 1, 2, 2, 2, 3, 3, 3, 3, 4, 4, 4, 5, 6, 6, 6, 6, 7, 7, 7, 8, and 9.

12. Any problem with 59 or greater as the top number could give you two different answers by flipping the subtrahend.

13. You can never have both the 2 and the 3 together in the top number.

14. Only three of the twelve problems had a 9 in the bottom number, because having 9 as the first digit in the bottom number is impossible.

15. Any problem with a 9 in the top number can have the bottom number reversed for a new problem that will work, except for subtracting from 39. For example 95 – 32 is different from 95 – 23; 93 – 25 is different from 93 – 52.

16. Every answer is greater than 5.

17. The range of the answers is between 6 and 72.

18. There are both odd and even answers.

19. If you add all the answers, you get 460.

20. You can make six pairs of answers that are all multiples of 10. I think you can pair each answer with another answer and end up with six multiples of 20.

This is a real range of discoveries! Some of them are much more mathematically significant than others. That's okay. Teachers need to honor the range of thinking, make it clear that any problem can be looked at in many ways, not make a big deal over those answers that are more complex or elegant than others. The classroom is a community of learners. Most children can automatically tell you who the best math students are, and I don't want to reinforce that. I want my students to feel that it is more important to contribute than to come up with the most complex idea. Children who take risks and add to the classroom pool of knowledge are more likely to continue doing this out of habit.

However, I am not in the business of enhancing children's self-esteem at the expense of accuracy. I talk about answers that are wrong, and I correct them. I do think it is important to point out wrong answers in a nonjudgmental way: *I don't agree. I noticed that you thought all the answers were two digits, but Kate said that she had 6 as an answer. Although you had ten answers, I noticed that some other children had a dozen.* I am disturbed that the current emphasis on problem solving is being construed as "all answers are correct." While it is true that I care about thinking and process, I want children to know that there are many kinds of problems. Some have multiple answers, some have one answer, most have more than one way to arrive at a solution. I also want the class to know that sometimes great thinking nevertheless includes a glitch that produces a wrong answer. Or, conversely, that sometimes faulty thinking still produces a correct answer. A classroom in which students feel excitement about mathematics and regularly converse about problems is an environment safe enough for a child (or a teacher!) to be wrong.

Venn Diagrams

At one time, set theory and Venn diagrams were discussed at the beginning of many fifth-grade textbooks, often as a way to introduce ideas of similarity and difference. Then this topic got moved nearer the middle of the book and finally to the end. It has disappeared altogether from many recent texts.

Being able to organize your thinking and analyze attributes and characteristics is a very valuable skill. Knowing what something is and is not is fundamental to logical thinking. Doctors use this kind of thinking when they compare symptoms with what they know about diseases and illnesses. This kind of reasoning is the underpinning of artificial intelligence (though what I am striving for in class is genuine intelligence). Older students use this kind of reasoning and categorization to determine whether a square is a rectangle (it is) or a rectangle is a square (not necessarily) and to think about real numbers, imaginary numbers, irrational numbers, rational numbers, and integers. This type of exercise may seem very basic for a fifth grader, but it is a very useful one.

I begin by playing a number of games in class. First I lay out a large circle on the floor with heavy cord and ask all the boys (or all the children who wear glasses or who have an older sister or who live in a brick house) to step inside the circle. Then I take that circle away and lay out two overlapping circles and assign each of them an attribute: for example, children who have freckles step into one of the circles, those with sneakers step into the other. It quickly becomes clear that both the intersection of the circles (for children who possess both attributes) and the area outside both circles (for children with neither attribute) are important. Sometimes I put children into the circles and ask the students to try to determine the categories I had in mind. Eventually I make these activities more representational, drawing circles on the board and writing students' names in them.

There are two parts to the ensuing homework assignment. The first involves a Venn diagram containing three rings, each labeled with a category related to characteristics of numbers between one and a hundred. (Possible categories are square numbers, numbers that are multiples of five, numbers that have a smaller tens digit than ones digit, numbers whose digits sum to nine, numbers whose digits are the same, odd numbers, prime numbers, numbers that are not multiples of three, numbers that begin with a consonant when they are spelled as words.) After labeling the three rings, I choose a range of numbers, say from 1 to 15; the students' job is to put those numbers in the correct place in the Venn diagram. There are many strategies for doing this, and I find I have to examine the numbers very carefully. When the homework assignments come in, I ask the children to compare their work. This is one of those clear-cut cases in which there is only one correct way to organize the numbers; however, the children's discussions defending their choices are passionate and reasoned. Figure 3.2 is an example of one such completed assignment.

The second part of the assignment, which comes from *Family Math* (Stenmark et al. 1986), is far more difficult and involves several blank Venn diagrams (see figure 3.3). Box 2 has two circles that do not intersect; the children are to

FIGURE 3.2   *A Completed Venn Diagram Assignment*

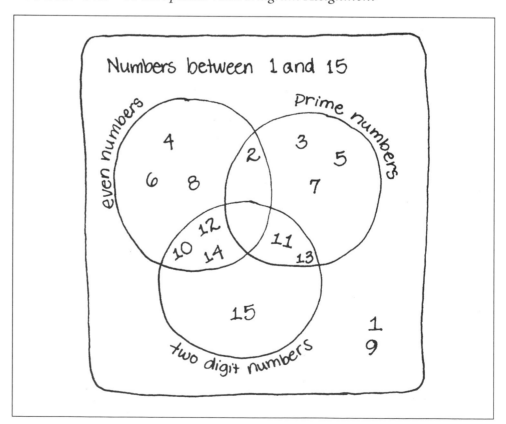

FIGURE 3.3 *A Blank Venn Diagram Assignment*

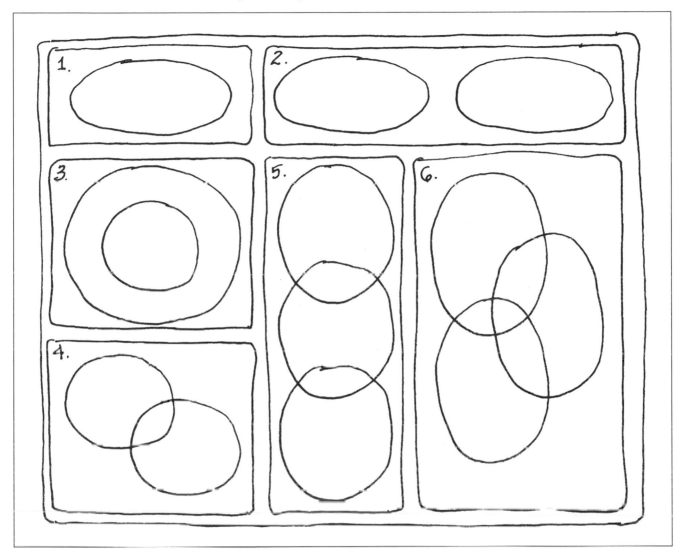

enter two categories that are mutually exclusive, that have no intersection: animals and plants, living and nonliving, male and female, solid and liquid, for example. Box 3 has two circles, one inside the other, the smaller a subcategory of the larger. All the items in the subcategory will belong to the general category, but not all items in the general category will belong to the subcategory. Things that might be entered in these circles include places in the United States and places in Massachusetts, and human beings and children. Boxes 4 and 6 are traditional versions incorporating two rings and three rings. Box 5 is the most difficult of all, a chain with three rings. Something can belong to the first and second category, or the second and third category, but never simultaneously to the first and third category.

My students have come up with interesting suggestions for what to place in the chain diagram. Hannah thought three categories that could work are *hard candy*, *sour candy*, and *chewy candy*, reasoning that candy could be sour and hard or sour and chewy but that no hard candy could also be chewy. Colin (see figure 3.4) suggested the three circles could be labeled *likes Legos*, *likes the color blue*, *hates Legos*. Sarah (see figure 3.5) suggested *flying animals*, *mammals*, and *walking animals*.

This is not an easy assignment to discuss or to correct. Some kids really get the idea, others are totally confused by the difference between an attribute and a specific example of that attribute. It's sometimes difficult to decide whether a difficult assignment like this is worth the time and effort, but since this kind of thinking is such a crucial part of higher mathematics and scientific reasoning, I'm convinced it is. But I'm glad not all the homework I give is this "fuzzy"!

FIGURE 3.4 *Colin's Solutions*

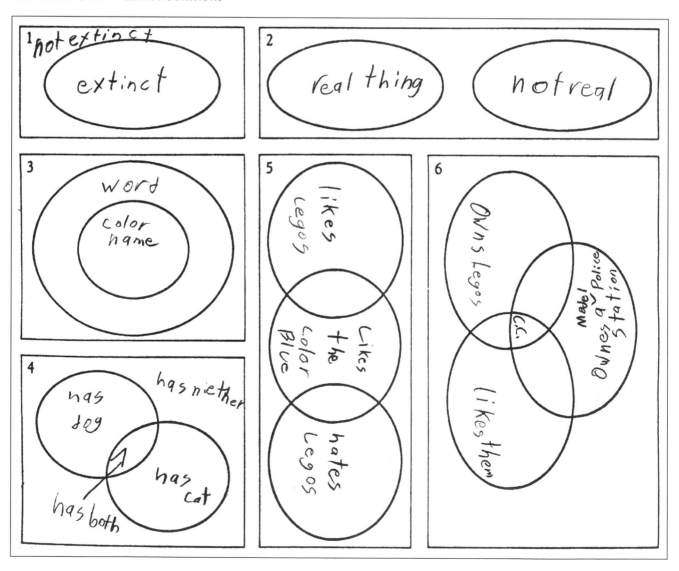

FIGURE 3.5 *Sarah's Solutions (some are incorrect)*

It's important that mathematics join the realm of shared school experiences. Interestingly, when you walk into schools, you often see displays of literacy or thematic studies. You much less often see displays of mathematical work. A school should work hard at ensuring a balance of disciplines celebrated in shared space, whether that be on a bulletin board or during an assembly.

This homework assignment grew out of a special mathematics assembly in which my whole school participated. We wanted to show that mathematics is part of every discipline, even music, and that it is helpful to have reference points for large numbers. There are, of course, other ways to establish a context for this assignment (you could, for example, read *On the Day You Were Born*, by Deborah Frasier). But I'm going to describe the assembly for you, because schools regularly have assemblies to showcase music or drama, a historical period, or an aspect of science, but rarely think about recreational mathematics for the entire school

When Will You Be Ten Thousand Days Old?

community. Doing mathematics outside the classroom is a valid way to model that it is part of the larger world and that it can be a common pleasurable experience. (If your school is too large for all the students to participate, you can still arrange a group experience for a number of classes.)

My small school includes children from kindergarten through sixth grade, and planning any mathematical event that will engage them all isn't easy. We've had students put a color-coded Unifix cube (each grade level is given a different color) in each of their pockets before coming to assembly, then deposit them in big buckets; the cubes were later counted and tallied to find out how many pockets there were in school that day and which grade level was wearing clothes with the most pockets. We've given each student a playing card and had everyone stand, first eliminating red cards, then clubs, then face cards, etc., until only children holding the six of spades remained standing. (This wasn't a totally successful activity for the kindergartners, but they didn't care; they loved all the standing and sitting.) We've shared mathematical poetry, sung songs with numbers in them, and had number quizzes (*How many bears slept in the house visited by Goldilocks?*). Once we transferred the terrific book *Only One*, by Marc Harshmann, onto overhead transparencies and the whole school responded to the book's questions regarding groups of things that yielded one (nine players make one team, for example).

The particular assembly I want to tell you about took place on January 9, 1993. First, the music teacher and a guitar-playing fifth-grade teacher came to the front of the room and led us in a rendition of the song "Inchworm." (To refresh your memory, the lyrics for one of the verses are: *Inchworm, Inchworm / Measuring the marigolds / You and your arithmetic / Will probably go far / Inchworm, Inchworm / Measuring the marigolds / Seems to me / You'd stop and see / How beautiful they are / Two and two are four / Four and four are eight / Eight and eight are sixteen / Sixteen and sixteen are thirty-two.*)

After we finished the song, I talked a little about doubling. Then, using an overhead calculator to verify our work, we began with one and kept doubling the number. Our goal was to reach 10,000. Doubling the one- and two-digit numbers was easy, especially since we'd just gone through most of them in the song. Then it began to get a little more difficult. But there was no lack of enthusiastic volunteers. Younger children raised their hand until the number got too large for them, then the older children took up the slack, thinking out loud until the number had reached 8,192. At this point we decided to round up to 10,000, because it was clear that the next number would be much bigger than our target.

Then we talked about ways we could think about the number 10,000. What equations or expressions could we come up with that would equal this number? Again, hands went up as students offered suggestions ranging from the easy (10,000 + 0) to the complicated (10 to the fourth power; X vinculum). (X vinculum is the roman numeral X with a line above it; the line indicates that whatever is under it is to be multiplied by 1,000. I didn't know this at the time, I'm ashamed to say, but our fifth graders, who were studying roman numerals, did!) Students posited equations using addition, subtraction, multiplication, and, after I pushed them a little, division.

Next I asked ten teachers to join me at the front of the room; each one held up a thousand cube from a set of base 10 blocks. We compared those ten larger cubes with one tiny centimeter cube and decided it would take 10,000 of the small cubes to make up the ten larger cubes.

Then I announced that the next day one of these teachers would be exactly 10,000 days old. I told the students that after a few minutes I would walk behind the row of teachers, pausing behind each one, and that they were to clap when they thought I was behind the person who was about to celebrate the 10,000-day milestone. (I used a wand made out of a ruler to which I'd attached a big star and some eye-catching silver ribbon streamers to add to the excitement.)

This activity challenged the students' number sense. (You may want to pause here a minute and figure out how many years 10,000 days are!) The teachers at the front of the auditorium were of varying ages. The assistant principal, who was the oldest of the group and had white hair, got a lot of votes, because 10,000 is a big number. Three other teachers also got votes. Then I asked the person who was going to be 10,000 days old to step forward, and Ms. Sullivan, our youngish (if, like me, your twenties were decades ago) science teacher did so.

A fierce discussion erupted about whether this was reasonable. Many students also wanted to know the date of Ms. Sullivan's birth. So we decided to work the problem on the overhead calculator. First, we divided 10,000 by 365 days, and got 27.39726. Thinking about .39726 of a year was too difficult, but the calculator was also able to report quotients with a remainder: this gave us 27 years, with 145 days left over.

But we'd forgotten about leap years! I put up a list of 27 full years, starting with 1965, and circled each leap year in red. There were seven, so we subtracted the 7 days that had been "used up" by leap years from the 145 days. Twenty-seven years of 365 days, with 7 more days to account for leap years, gave us a total of 9,862 days. Now we had to account for the remaining 138 days. We subtracted 9 days to account for the nine days of January that had passed since 1993 began. That mean that 129 days prior to the end of 1965 would be Ms. Sullivan's birthday. We subtracted 31 from 129 to account for the month of December, leaving 98 days. Subtracting the 30 days of November left 68 days, minus October's 31 days left 37 days, minus September's 30 days left 7 days. Counting backward seven days from the end of August, we arrived at August 24th, which was indeed Ms. Sullivan's birthday. (The 24th itself doesn't count, because you aren't 1 day old until 24 hours have passed. Therefore, August 25, 26, 27, 28, 29, 30, and 31 are the seven days in August.)

The investigation about the 10,000th day proved to be very powerful and led to several homework experiences. A fifth-grade class decided to investigate the number 10,000 in three different ways: pennies (how many dollars would you have if you put a penny in a jar each day for 10,000 days?), ounces (how many one-pound bags of one-ounce Milky Way bars would you have if you set aside a one-ounce Milky Way bar each day for 10,000 days?), and inches (how many five-feet-six-inches-tall people could lie head to foot in a space 10,000 inches long?).

Each sixth grader figured out the day that he or she would celebrate their 10,000th day alive and wrote about the strategies (and shortcuts) they had used (figure 3.6 is one example). (Raquel looked at a calendar that indicated what day of the year it was and thus eliminated lots of work!) This was, mercifully, a self-correcting assignment! When they posted the results on a class chart, there were giggles when two students born a day apart predicted 10,000-day celebrations half

FIGURE 3.6   *A Sixth Grader Discovers When She Will Be 10,000 Days Old*

The way I figured out that I would turn 10,000 days on September 26, 2008 is I knew that I would be 27 (since Ms. Sullivan was) so I multiplied 27×365 and I got 9855. Then I added six days on for leap years and I got 9861. 10,000 subtract 9861 equals 139. Last I kept on subtracting the days of the month from my birthday so there were 11 days in March, 30 in April, 31 in May, June, July, and August, and 4 days in September. That gave me my answers

a year apart and cheers when two students born the same day came up with the same date. The intricacies of leap years were much discussed, especially whether one had been born before or after the extra day. And there was even some speculation about whether any of the teachers in school might be 20,000 days old!

Additional Extension
Homework Assignments

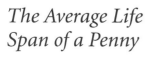

The Average Life Span of a Penny

EMPHASIS: *data collection and analysis*

Get a roll of pennies from the bank (or collect 50 pennies from your family members) and graph the pennies' "birth dates." Predict what the same graph done a year from now would look like.

EMPHASIS: *data collection and analysis*

NOTE: You'll need to purchase a box of animal crackers for everyone in the class, which you can do inexpensively at warehouse distribution centers like BJ's and Sam's Club. Alternatively, if it is acceptable in your community, you can ask parents to provide a box for their child. (You can also adapt this activity to a can of mixed nuts, a roll of multicolored lifesavers, or a bag of assorted gumdrops.)

How many different animals are in a box of animal crackers? How many are there of each? Are there the same number of bears as elephants? Figure out a way to record the contents of the box. Then write a letter to the manufacturer and tell them what you found.

Lions and Tigers and Bears

EMPHASIS: *organizing data, finding patterns*

NOTE: Dominoes come in double-six, double-nine, and double-twelve sets. This activity requires either running off facsimile domino sets on card stock, cutting them into individual pieces, and putting each set in a baggie or envelope (which is a lot of work!) or having access to enough real sets so every child can take home a set for a night or two during a given period.

Find a way to figure out the total number of dots (also called pips) there are in a set of dominoes without actually counting the dots. Are there patterns that will help you?

Domino Dots

EMPHASIS: *collecting information, problem solving*

How long would it take the students in your school to drink 1,000,000 pints of milk? What is the average number of pints consumed each day? How many school days are there in one year? How much milk is that, anyway?

A Million Pints of Milk

EMPHASIS: *data collection, mathematics in a real-world context*

Cut out a paragraph from an article in a newspaper or magazine. Examine the first 100 letters. Construct a graph of which letters appear how many times. Combine your graph with those of the other students in your class. What do you see about the frequency of letters in the English language? What does this have to do with math, anyway? How might you use this information?

One Hundred Letters

Math
Homework
Emphasizing
Creativity

It's high time to dispel the myth that there is no room for creativity in mathematics. Because computers and calculators perform most of the arithmetic in the real world, we desperately need people who understand numbers and their relationships. Technology allows us to plug numbers into a formula and come out with a precise, accurate, reliable answer. What we need are students capable of coming up with the formulas! We need to encourage innovative thinking in students who have a deep understanding of numbers, especially their relationships to other numbers. Our students must be able to generalize about mathematical processes, cut big problems down into smaller chunks, and represent their thinking.

Whenever I made a creative math assignment, I used to worry that certain children would be paralyzed by these open-ended opportunities or would feel bad when they compared their work with the work of their peers. But I've found that the benefits of projects like this outweigh the possible negatives. More often than not, my students, across the board, exceed my expectations.

My impetus to increase the number of creative assignments I gave came from the responses of two very different students. Jim struggled with math and found the basics difficult and frustrating: coming to my math class required a daily act of courage! Yet he enjoyed the creative projects, because they were based as much on effort as they were on ability. With the help and encouragement of his father, he eagerly put effort, thought, and time into the creative projects I assigned and basked in the respect he got from me and his peers when he turned them in. They

were a real oasis for him. On the other hand, Mike was one of the most talented children I have ever taught; his conceptual base and intellectual understanding often exceeded my own. Much of what I was teaching in class was a review of what he already knew. He also loved the creative projects, because he used them to deal with mathematically rigorous problems or experiments that let him, as he said, "sink my teeth into math."

One way that I keep in touch with how students are feeling about their work is through journals. If a project seems overwhelming, a journal gives students a private way to let me know: they will write things there they would never say to my face (how annoyed they are when a classmate proclaims that something they are finding difficult is easy, their secret admiration of the way another student has solved a problem). Journals let me check in as my students struggle with larger projects. When I write back to them (I often type my response on my computer, print it out on a label, and then paste it in their journal), I am establishing a personal connection.

Sometimes I give a structured journal assignment, but my standing invitation to my students is simply to share what's on their mind. They may complain about test questions, comments I've made in class, or a written evaluation. They may thank me for feedback on a paper or an assignment. They may wonder what probability, dice rolling, or geometry has to do with math. Sometimes they may pass along the skepticism or approval of their parents.

The feedback I've received over the years has made me realize that creative assignments are very important. They allow a wide variety of children to get involved. They allow me to see what happens when we go beyond the normal confines of the curriculum. Parents are almost always more aware of creative assignments than they are of more mundane ones. Students who have only a mild affection for mathematics can direct these assignments toward their own interests.

Schooling is something of a blur for children. As much as we may hate to admit it, they remember the big events—the field trips, the plays, the recitals, the assemblies. Very rarely are these big events related to their math learning. Some of them need to be.

That being said, there is one major caveat: don't bite off more than you can chew. Once, inspired by Gary Tsuruda, author of *Putting It Together* (1994), who challenged his class to explain a branch of mathematics in a way that "no textbook would ever have the guts to," I assigned one of my classes a project about percents. When the videos, scripts, games, children's books, newspapers, and puzzles came in, I piled them in a crate, afraid to look at them. Why had I made such an open-ended assignment? Checking for the correct answers on a worksheet would have been so much easier. And the students naturally wanted the projects back right away—after all, look at all the time they'd invested. The good news is that after getting over my terror and making it clear to myself and my students that it would take me a while to give the projects the attention they deserved, I actually enjoyed going through them. And I gained a new respect for my students' talent and creativity. But I also learned my limits: there's only so much time I can spend grading big, long-term assignments. I continue to give a variety of creative assignments, but they are not all huge productions.

Example Activities

Cooperative Cards

To introduce this homework assignment, I gave each group of four students ten number tiles with the digits 0 through 9 on them and told them to spread out the tiles in order so that they could all see. I then gave each group a deck of four special cards I'd prepared, one for each member of the group. (The backs of each deck of four cards were coded so that it was easy to keep the decks separate.) I asked each child to follow the directions on her or his card, which had to do with taking away some of the tiles. After everyone had done what his or her card asked, only one tile would remain. They could read the cards to one another in any order, discuss what the directions might mean, and ask questions. They might even discover that some of the tiles would fit the conditions on more than one card, but each person would always be able to remove at least one tile. My one stipulation was that they couldn't let anyone else *see* their card. (I wanted to promote working as a group and encourage students to listen to one another.)

Here are the directions for fourteen sets of cards appropriate for young intermediate students:

Set 1:

Take away any even numbers.

Take away any numbers greater than the number of days in a week.

Take away the number equal to the number of fingers you have on one hand.

Take away any numbers made from only straight lines.

Set 2:

Take away numbers less than 4 + 4.

Take away any numbers that begin with the letter *s* when they are written as words.

Take away any even numbers.

Take away any numbers that are less than half of 10.

Set 3:

Take away any numbers that are greater than the number of days in a week.

Take away any numbers that are less than the number of sides on a square.

Take away any number you say when you count by threes.

Take away the two consecutive numbers (next to each other) that add up to nine.

Set 4:

Take away any numbers greater than the number of cents in a nickel.

Take away any number you say when you count by two.

Take away zero.

Take away any numbers that have curves in them.

Set 5:

Take away any numbers that include an i when they are spelled as words.

Take away any numbers that are less than the number of legs a dog has.

Take away any number equal to the number of legs on two people.

Take away any numbers that begin with a vowel when they are spelled as words.

Set 6:

Take away the number equal to the number of cents in a penny; then, if you can, also take away the number equal to the number of cents in a nickel.

Take away any numbers greater than the number of colored lights on a standard traffic light.

Take away the number equal to the number of sides on a triangle.

Take away the number equal to the number of shoes in a pair.

Set 7:

If you can, take away the number equal to the number of sides on one square; then take away the number equal to the number of sides on two squares.

Take away any numbers smaller than half a dozen.

Take away any numbers that begin with the letter s when they are spelled as words.

Take away any numbers that begin with the letter t when they are spelled as words.

Set 8:

Take away any numbers that begin with the letter f when they are spelled as words.

Take away any numbers that contain less than four letters when they are spelled as words.

Take away any number that is one more than 6.

Take away any number that includes a closed region (if you put up a fence in the shape of the number, there would be a place in which to put an animal so it could not get away).

Set 9:

Take away any number that does not use the letter e when it is spelled as a word.

Take away the number that is one less than 10.

Take away any numbers less than 6.

Take away any number that begins with the letter s when it is spelled as a word.

Set 10:

Take away any numbers that include the letter v when they are spelled as a word.

Take away the number equal to the number of noses on your face.

Take away any numbers that are even.

Take away any numbers that are greater than the largest number you can find on a single die.

Set 11:

Take away any numbers smaller than the number equal to the number of sides on a triangle.

Take away any number you don't say when you count by twos.

Take away the number equal to the number of wheels most passenger cars have.

Take away the number equal to the number of sides on a stop sign.

Set 12:

Take away any numbers that contain exactly four letters when they are spelled as words.

Take away any odd numbers.

Take away the number equal to the number of seasons in a year.

Take away any numbers that are greater than 5 and less than 9.

Set 13:

Take away the numbers that mean first or second.

Take away any numbers that contain more than four letters when they are spelled as words.

Take away any number that includes the letter *z* when it is spelled as a word.

Take away any numbers that include the letter *i* when they are spelled as words.

Set 14:

Take away the number equal to the number of wheels on three bicycles; then take away the number equal to the number of wheels on three tricycles.

Take away any numbers that include the letter *o* when they are spelled as words.

Take away the number that is equal to half of 6.

Take away any numbers that are greater than 6 and less than 9.

My fourth graders had fun with this activity, but most of them agreed that the mathematics was not too difficult.

I then explained that I had created these cards by first writing down the digits from 0 through 9. Knowing I had exactly four chances to get rid of nine out of the ten digits, I wrote a clue, crossed out the digits that would be taken away, and used the remaining digits to give me ideas for each subsequent clue.

Next we brainstormed what kinds of things would be appropriate clues for fourth graders: the answers to computation problems, factors or multiples of a number, numbers used in real-life contexts, consecutive numbers, the numerator or denominator of a fraction. Although the students were comfortable about mentioning areas that were new to them (factors and fractions, for example), few actually used these ideas when working on their own.

Then I asked them to reconvene their groups of four, spread out their ten tiles, and, using four 3-by-5-inch file cards, write four clues that would get rid of all but one digit. I cautioned them not to start out by deciding which digit they wanted to remain but to be flexible and keep writing clues to eliminate digits until one remained.

This is a difficult task, because the clues are supposed to work in any order. (Some of my examples are better than others in this regard.) There was some confusion, but groups settled down to the task and asked for help when they knew they were in trouble.

The following day, we finished writing our cooperative tile riddles and exchanged them with one another, first establishing some ground rules for how to give sensitive, helpful feedback. We wanted to discover which clues were successful and which ones were ambiguous and needed changing. (I wish I'd had that kind of feedback when I was writing my own cards!)

For homework, each child, individually, had one week to write exactly four clues to get rid of nine digits. Here are some student originals:

Take away any two digits that when added together are eight less than half of the number of letters in the alphabet.

Take away all the odd numbers.

Take away the number equal to a half dozen.

Take away the three smallest even numbers.

Take out all the even numbers that don't include the letter *i* when written as a word.

Take out the factors of 27.

Take out all even numbers greater than 6.

Take out all the odd numbers less than 9.

Take away the smallest counting number.

Take away all the even numbers.

Take away half the number of letters in the alphabet minus 6.

Take away the two numbers that together are the answer to 19×5.

Take away all even numbers.

Take away the number you get when you divide 27 by 3.

Take away all the factors of 7.

Take away the number you get when you divide 6 by 2.

Take away the number that you can multiply by itself and get the same number.

Take away all the even numbers.

Take away $[(7 \times 6) - 2]$ divided by 8.

Take away all multiples of 3.

I think this is an especially powerful experience for children. It lets them really key into their own number sense and familiarity with numbers. I especially like this assignment because before they do it on their own for homework, they get the support of a group while they do it in class. Working on something as a group helps them see that each person holds important pieces of information and that they can be better problem solvers together than they can be alone. Their in-class experience giving helpful feedback teaches them how to monitor their own progress and look critically at their own work before I ever see it. Obviously, homework can't be cooperative: children don't always have the time or the means to get together. Nevertheless, an assignment like this, which will eventually be solved by a group of children, reinforces the idea that some of what happens in math class should be collaborative.

I also appreciate the slight disdain my students always show for my examples, which are neither as challenging nor as mathematical as they ought to be. This seems to spur many of them on to write problems more indicative of their talents and more worthy of their attention. That's fine with me!

I use the problems they have written on the occasions when I invite parents into the classroom. Although mathematics also involves shapes and measurement, I tend to involve parents in something having to do with numbers, since that's what they are most interested in, what many of them consider to be "true" mathematics. Parents get to know one another as they work with these cards, and they gain a real respect for their children's thinking. Many can't believe that children in the intermediate grades are capable of this kind of complex understanding. Now and then I invite groups of parents to write cooperative cards for the class. In doing so, they realize that it is far from trivial to use up nine digits in four clues. The children enjoy doing the problems their parents leave behind, and my own stack of cooperative problems increases.

Historically, the cost of sending a first-class letter via the United States Postal Service has been:

November 3, 1917	3 cents
July 1, 1919	2 cents
July 6, 1932	3 cents
August 1, 1958	4 cents
January 7, 1963	5 cents
January 7, 1968	6 cents
May 16, 1971	8 cents
March 2, 1974	10 cents
December 31, 1975	13 cents
May 29, 1978	15 cents
March 22, 1981	18 cents
November 1, 1981	20 cents
February 17, 1985	22 cents
April 3, 1988	25 cents
February 3, 1991	29 cents
January 1, 1995	32 cents
January 10, 1999	33 cents

Neither Rain Nor Snow Nor Dark of Night

Last year I gave this information to my students and asked them, as a homework assignment, to predict the price of a stamp in the year 2010. I was amazed at the diversity of opinions. Some students talked about the difficulty choosing kinds of stamps (Elvis vs. Love stamps, for example), which has little to do with mathematics. Some said that past trends would change because of email and faxes. Some discounted anything before 1978, because the value of money in the last two decades has changed so drastically. Some looked at the price of a stamp each decade. Some graphed the date and the price of a stamp without taking into account a difference in the intervals between price changes (thirteen years before the first increase in the price of a stamp, as opposed to four years before the last increase). One of my students found the difference between each new price and the date on which the change was made (for example, the difference between 2—the cost of the stamp—and 1—the day in July when the price increased—is 1; the difference between 3—the cost of the stamp—and 6—the day in July when the price increased—is 3) and then found the average of those numbers. My good friend Ruth Cossey calls this kind of mathematical thinking "voodoo math," because there is no reasoning, simply meaningless arithmetic computation.

Coleman came into class with his assignment and said, in his typical Eeyore way, "So, Mrs. Raphel, what's the right answer?" I laughed. This was a problem we wouldn't know the answer to until 2010!

However, we graphed all of our predictions to look at the range of responses (from no change to 54 cents) and surveyed other classes to see how we compared. We looked at the mean, the mode, and the median of our guesses; we discussed theories; and we talked about how we probably couldn't figure this out purely mathematically but had to take into account a little history and a little economics.

Recently one of my former students sent me a wonderful cartoon that depicts two people in front of a computer screen looking at an on-line headline about the rise in stamp prices. The caption says, "What's a stamp?"

All About Rice

Yang the Youngest and His Terrible Ear, by Lensey Namioka, has a wonderful passage that one year prompted a mathematical extravaganza in my school's fourth-grade mathematics classes:

> Looking first at me and then at Matthew, Mother smiled. "Since there are two of you to help carry, I'll buy a big sack of rice this time—a fifty-pound bag."
>
> Even with two of us, we were panting hard when we finally heaved the sack of rice into the bus. Matthew didn't believe me at first when I told him that we would eat up all the rice in about two months.

I borrowed a 50-pound bag of rice from the school kitchen so the students could see what it looked like. First the students listed everything they thought they already knew about rice, including where and how it was grown and how it might be prepared. Then they asked questions they thought they might like to investigate.

> How many grains are in a pound of rice?
> How many pieces of rice are in 50 pounds?
> What is the size of one piece of rice?
> How many teaspoons of rice are in 50 pounds?
> How long would it take to eat 50 pounds of rice?

How much does a 50-pound bag of rice cost?

Where does rice grow?

What country grows the most rice?

Is rice good for you? How?

Is it possible for one person to eat 50 pounds of rice?

How long would it take to fill one bag?

How long a line would it make if the rice in a 50-pound bag was laid end to end?

How many bowlsful of rice are in a 50-pound bag?

How long would it take to count the rice in a 50-pound bag?

How long would it take to clean it up if it was spilled?

How much does a grain of rice weigh?

We then talked about which questions could be investigated in the classroom (*How many grains are in a pound of rice?*) and which could be answered by doing research in a textbook (*What country grows the most rice?*).

Next I asked the students to predict how many grains they thought were in the bag. The range of responses was enormous, and each person recorded his or her guess on a strip of paper. We put the strips in order from the smallest guess to the largest and used the opportunity to talk about place value and comparing large numbers. Then, in groups of four, the children investigated how they might determine how many grains were actually in the 50-pound bag and recorded their methods on a file card. (As any teacher knows, pushing words around to get them to say exactly what you mean in a way your audience can understand is laborious. Children are eager to take shortcuts. Communicating fully takes time, patience, and persistence.)

As a first step, most of the groups measured rice in a cup, divided it up among the four members of their group, and then counted the grains. Others counted the number of grains in a smaller measurement (one eighth teaspoon, one tablespoon, one ounce, or one-eighth cup). The next step, figuring out how many grains were in a pound (which, multiplied times 50, would tell them how many grains were in the bag), was attempted in a number of ways, among them weighing a cup of rice and consulting a table of measurement equivalents. The conversation as the quartets tried to make sense of the open-ended task, as they came up with implausible answers, as their fragile understanding led them to dead ends, or as they carefully retraced steps to make sure they did not get lost in the intricate web of their complex thinking, was energetic and focused.

The range of responses to how many grains of rice there were in a 50-pound bag was very wide—from a low estimate of 301,600 to a high estimate of 1,443,000. This was okay. It's important to feel comfortable with ambiguity. Besides, when you extrapolate data from a small sample, a small error gets multiplied many, many times. The wide span gave us an excellent opportunity to talk about what variables could account for the differences, which methods seemed more credible than others, which numbers made the most sense and why. We also talked about the precision of the measuring instruments themselves, how those made by different manufacturers can have slightly different capacities! (The September 1999 issue of *Gourmet Magazine*, on page 32, highlights the capacity variations in brands of measuring spoons!)

The final part of this assignment allowed the children to investigate something they themselves cared about. I encouraged them to go back to their original list of questions for inspiration. Their mission was to ask a question, do the research needed to arrive at the answer, and present the information (to include how the problem was solved) in the form of a poster on which the answer was concealed under a flap a passerby could lift to check his or her guess.

I was surprised and pleased by the range of intricate and imaginative questions the students came up with. (Most of them went well beyond our original list.) Here are some of them:

How many grains of rice can fit inside a size $6\frac{1}{2}$ shoe?
How many grains of rice would fit on one tile in the science room?
How many grains of rice would fit in a marker cap?
How much water would it take to cook all 50 pounds?
How much space would 50 pounds of rice occupy after it was cooked?
How long would it take the school to eat 50 pounds of rice?
How long would it take one person to cook 50 pounds of rice in a pot that can cook two cups at a time?
How many grains would fit inside a can of Pepsi?
How many times could you write the word *word* using rice grains?

These investigations required time, patience, and careful listening. Children got tangled up in their thinking and I needed to ask questions (gently, of course) to help them with their reasoning. However, there were rich opportunities to introduce mathematics in context. Was it worth the amount of time it took? I say a resounding yes. This kind of deep mathematical experience models the way in which real problem solvers approach real challenges.

The long-term homework assignment related to this investigation was to find out how many of something else there are in fifty pounds: how many Cheerios? how many sneakers? how many pencils? how many jellybeans? how many dollar bills? how many computer disks? how many house keys? how many textbooks? It culminated in a bulletin-board display that included one each of the objects children chose to investigate, the number of each object there are in 50 pounds, and the mathematical computation and thinking the student had used to arrive at the answer. The posters were ready for back-to-school night, and the students' parents were impressed with their children's thinking and their ability to articulate their strategies. They developed a healthy respect for the magnitude of numbers and for the complexity of the math that their children were studying. Parental approval of our school's mathematics program so early in the year yielded rich partnerships for the remainder of it.

An activity like this, involving something fairly small and inexpensive, is a good way to start the year, provided it includes class brainstorming before children are asked to do any independent investigation. (Another year, for example, we were reading *Mine for Keeps*, by Jean Little, a story about a Seeing Eye dog. We got a 50-pound bag of dog food and did the same kind of thing. Children investigated how many kibbles it would take to go across the United States, how long the bag would last if it was used to feed various-size dogs, etc. We also researched what it costs to own a dog, with individual students researching the cost of a leash, a visit to the vet, grooming supplies, registration at town hall, and so forth.) In addition to the benefits of being able to display the posters during parent night, beginning the year with an activity like this helps you avoid starting off with review sheets and tests. Instead of finding out what children already know using some artificially constructed chapter test or criterion-referenced evaluation, I find out lots by informally observing the way a child or group of children works. The children are engaged, and I have time to walk around, watching, listening, and taking notes. My students get the message that mathematics is more than naked arithmetic, that they can do math with markers and newsprint as well as with worksheets. It sets up expectations that math will have interesting contexts, that it will be responsive to their interests, that it can be approached in lots of ways, that I prize ownership of ideas, and that I don't have all the answers (much less the questions!) tucked away in a teacher's manual.

To lead up to the eventual homework assignment (which is also discussed in another Math Solutions Publications book, *Getting Your Math Message Out to Parents,* by Nancy Litton), I devoted a class period to having the students rotate through fourteen "estimation centers" I had set up throughout the room. (These activities were inspired by those suggested in the Family Math program, which was developed by the Equals staff at the University of California's Lawrence Hall of Science.) Each center asked the students (in pairs) to make an estimate of some kind. There was a clue card at each center to help them get started. The fourteen centers, each with the respective clue card, follow.

Estimation Centers

1. Description: At this station, there were 30 pennies in a translucent film container. Next to the container were 10 loose pennies that the children could manipulate.
   Activity: **Estimate how many pennies are in the container.**
   Clue: *Does it help to make a stack of ten pennies?*

2. Description: This station contained a balance scale, a pair of giant dice, and 11 cubes. The scale came close to balancing with one die and 9 or 10 cubes, but there were not enough cubes to balance both dice.
   Activity: **Estimate how many cubes will balance the dice.**
   Clue: *You can pick up the cubes and the dice in your hands. You can use the scale too!*

3. Description: At this station there were a three-minute timer and a stopwatch. The children were not given enough time to wait for all the sand in the timer to empty, but they could time how long it took for a portion of the sand to empty. (Note: Not many students were aware that it was probably a three-minute timer; those who were seemed to be interested in seeing whether it was accurate.)
   Activity: **Estimate how long it will take for the sand in the timer to go down.**
   Clue: *Does it help to think about how long it will take for half of the sand to go down?*

4. Description: This station contained a box about five cubes wide and about ten cubes long. There were twelve cubes for the children to manipulate,

enough to lay them across the width of the box or down the length of it, but not enough to do both simultaneously.

Activity: **Estimate how many blocks will cover the bottom of the box.**

Clue: *Can you lay out the blocks on the bottom of the box to see how many will go across its width? Can you lay them out to see how many will go down its length?*

5. Description: This station contained a bowl of kidney beans, several small identical plastic cups, and several larger identical plastic cups. There were enough beans to fill a small cup about five times, but not enough to fill a large cup, which held about eight times the volume of a small cup.

   Activity: **Estimate how many little cups of beans fit into a big cup.**

   Clue: *Does it help to try to put a few small cups of beans into the large cup?*

6. Description: This station had a very thick piece of licorice that was twenty-five inches long. (There was a backup piece of the same length in a plastic bag.)

   Activity: **Estimate how long the licorice is.**

   Clue: *This card is 5 inches wide. Does that help you?*

7. Description: At the station were a stack of 125 white cards and a smaller pile of 20 pink cards of the same size and shape.

   Activity: **Estimate how many white cards are in this stack.**

   Clue: *There are 20 pink cards in the small pile.*

8. Description: At this station were an unopened package of Necco Wafers and 10 loose ones. (Crackers or candy that is packed cylindrically would also work fine for this center.)

   Activity: **Estimate how many Necco Wafers are in the package.**

   Clue: *Don't count them. You may use the loose ones to help you.*

9. Description: At this station there were a large plastic mixing bowl and two identical glass canning jars (without markings on the side to show capacity). One of the jars had three cups of rice already in it and was sealed. The other jar was empty. A plastic bag held one cup of rice. There was also a funnel, as well as a one-cup measuring cup for verification purposes.

   Activity: **Estimate how many cups of rice are in a full jar.**

   Clue: *There is one cup of rice in this bag. Pour it into the empty jar. Use the bowl so you don't spill anything.*

10. Description: At this station was a standard canning jar with 414 lima beans inside. Next to it was a plastic bag containing 100 lima beans.

    Activity: **Estimate how many lima beans are in the jar.**

    Clue: *There are 100 lima beans in the plastic bag.*

11. Description: At this station were 15 wooden balls from a baby's game, each weighing about an ounce. There was also a kitchen scale.

    Activity: **Estimate how much these balls weigh.**

    Clue: *Don't take all the balls out. You may weigh one or a few of them.*

12. Description: For this station I had outlined a symmetric but intricate shape that would hold 42 tiles. (I folded a piece of one-inch graph paper in half and

cut along the lines in an intricate design, unfolded the shape, and traced carefully around it.) There were 15 tiles available to place inside the outline.
Activity: **Estimate the number of tiles it would take to fill this shape.**
Clue: *Try putting some of these tiles inside it. Are parts of the shape the same?*

13. Activity: **Estimate how tall Mrs. Raphel is.** (I was a little surprised when a pair of students who were estimating my height asked me to lay down on the floor because they felt distance on the floor was easier to estimate than vertical distance! Another pair asked me to stand back to back with another teacher, still another asked me to stand against the doorjamb.)
    Clue: *Think of how tall you are. Will that help?*

14. Description: At this station were a strip of paper 24 inches long and 13 plastic lima beans, each one inch long.
    Activity: **Estimate how many lima beans will fit across this paper.**
    Clue: *Can you figure out how many lima beans would fit across half the paper?*

I also gave the children an "answer sheet" containing a blank line for the estimate followed by the appropriate label (pennies, cubes, etc.). I did not provide a unit designation in cases where length was being measured, because I wanted to see how they would report it (centimeters? inches? yards?). In a little box at the bottom were two additional questions: *Which station was the most difficult? Which station was the least difficult?*

I orchestrated the movement from center to center by ringing a small bell and announcing that it was time to enter their estimate on their answer sheet and move to the next station. As I observed the children work together, discussing, handling the objects, reasoning, I was delighted with the strategies I saw emerging.

When everyone had finished, we had a very interesting discussion about hard and easy centers. We found there were great differences in what was thought to be easy and what was thought to be difficult. I brought up how much it hurts when someone is working very hard on a task and overhears another student say, "Oh, that was so easy!" Understanding that what is easy for one child may be difficult for another leads to greater sensitivity when talking about the challenge of a particular task.

At the end of the class period, I assigned the following homework:

Today in class we estimated different things, including height, length, time, amounts, and weight. For next Tuesday I would like you to complete a personal estimation project. Choose something you think would be fun to estimate. My ideas, which are seldom as interesting or as inventive as yours, include:

The number of grapes in a bunch.
How many times the refrigerator door opens in 24 hours at your house.
How many grocery items are in the cart when your mother or father gets to the grocery-store checkout.
How many cars pass by your house in a fifteen-minute period.
How many windows (or electrical outlets, or stair steps) are in your house.

How many words (or letter *es*) there are in a paragraph in the newspaper.

How many children in our class have a birthday in March

Write down your estimate before you actually gather the data. This is very important. Then gather the data to find out what the actual number or measurement is. Finally, in writing, tell me why you chose this particular thing to estimate, your strategy for making the estimate, what you did to gather the information to check your estimate, whether your estimate turned out to be a good one, and whether the answer is likely to be more or less the same or very different if you did the same activity again. (For example: Does the refrigerator door open more frequently on weekends than on weekdays? Would counting the windows in your house next week yield a different result? Does the number of grapes vary a lot from bunch to bunch?)

The children's ideas were indeed much more creative than the ones I had listed.

Patrick wrote, "I estimated that we changed the channel on the TV 26 times a day. We changed it 28 times a day. On a weekend, I estimated around 37 times a day. We changed it 73 times a day!"

Rory estimated how long it would take his brother to eat a chocolate egg. He guessed $2\frac{1}{2}$ minutes. It took 4 minutes and 14 seconds. He arrived at his estimate by taking the time it took him to eat one himself and adding to that half of the time it took his mom to eat one. But on the test his brother began by just nibbling at the chocolate and that took "a minute or so. After that I was way off." He concluded that his brother actually has two different styles: "He eats them whole when he's in a hurry but he nibbles it when he's relaxing."

Margaret guessed how many times her brother played Nintendo in two days. She estimated four times, but he didn't play at all. "I chose this question because my brother usually plays a lot. I thought he would play four times because he usually plays at least twice a day. I had no idea that those two days were going to be so hot."

Steve estimated that he had 80 stuffed animals in his house, and he actually had 73. He reported a difference of 7. "I always ask for a stuffed animal, but now that I know how many we have, I won't."

Linda was interested in how many times the phone rang in twenty-four hours. She estimated seven rings. There were really ten. "This project was interesting because it was difficult to estimate, plus Kim is on the phone a lot so it doesn't ring because maybe it is busy."

Rachel wanted to know how much junk mail they get and estimated ten pieces. "I estimated junk mail because I wanted to see how much paper we waste. Also it was convenient. My strategy was to think how much mail we got, so I could think what percent is junk mail. My estimate was good. There were 13 pieces."

Mary chose to estimate how many times the refrigerator opened in twenty-four hours. She guessed twenty-four, but it turned out to be thirty-four. She checked her estimate by putting a piece of paper on the refrigerator door and asking her family members to put a tally on the paper whenever they opened it. "If I did it again, it would turn out to be totally different. I do not eat as much as I did when I did it. My sister loved it so much that she even wanted to put away my apple juice. She never wants to do that!"

Additional Homework Assignments That Promote Creativity

The Water Project

NOTE: This activity will require conversations about data-collection strategies (Post-it notes? a clipboard? file cards?), a letter home, and a familiarity with different kinds of graphs, tables, and charts (for the presentation of the data). Allow lots of time for this in addition to the week in which students collect the data.

How much water do you use in one week? Figure out a way to keep track of your water consumption and present the data you collect in an interesting way. For example: Do you shower longer on some days than on others? Does your mother use more or less water than you do? How does water usage compare room by room (laundry room versus kitchen versus bathroom)? How does water usage compare in terms of the purpose it's used for (cleaning, cooking, personal hygiene)? You may want to contact your local public water authority for information about the average amount of water used to flush a toilet, brush one's teeth, do a load of laundry, etc.

Food Projects

Food (as we saw in the earlier activity using rice) lends itself naturally to some rich mathematical investigations. Pick a food and start asking questions.

Popcorn (see the Ideas column of the October 1990 *Arithmetic Teacher*)

How much more space does popcorn occupy after it is popped?

How many kernels are in a handful?

How many miniature paper cups will $\frac{1}{3}$ cup uncooked kernels fill?

How many popped kernels will fit in a one-cup measuring cup?

How much unpopped popcorn will yield one serving? (How much is one serving?)

How much popcorn would we need to feed 100 people? How many people can each student in our class invite to this gathering if everyone gets to invite the same number of guests and we want as close to 100 people as we can without going over?

Can you construct a container for one serving?

How much popcorn do Americans eat?

Compare unit prices of popcorn.

Rate three different kinds of popcorn for taste, affordability, and nutrition.

Compare and contrast microwave and standard popcorn.

Gather popcorn information from two local movie theaters and present what you find out in an interesting way.

Pizza (see the Ideas column of the April 1991 Arithmetic Teacher)

Take a survey of topping preferences in the class and display what you find out.

If a large pizza serves eight, a medium pizza serves six, and a small pizza serves two, what are some of the combinations that you could order to serve pizza to the whole class?

Compare and contrast pizza prices from different companies (frozen or retail).

Which is a better deal, a medium pizza or a large pizza? What information would you need in order to answer that question? Compare the areas of both and the prices. Are there other variables that would affect your answer?

How much does it cost to make a pizza? Make a list of all the ingredients and figure out what portion of each product is used to make a single pizza. From the cost of five pounds of flour, can you figure out the price for the number of cups of flour you actually use?

Other possible food topics include cereal, bread, cookies, ice cream, candy bars, and the information on nutrition labels.

Some of you will read this book from cover to cover; maybe you'll be inspired and energized, not so much by the ideas as by things my students have done and said. Others of you may scan the table of contents for something to use in your classroom tomorrow morning. Or maybe you'll photocopy a page to pass along to your principal or a colleague. Maybe you'll mention one of the activities in your school's newsletter. Maybe you'll put a copy of the book on the "parent" bookshelf. Maybe you'll decide that the ideas here are too much work or too difficult for your students or too hard to correct or too different from what you, your administrator, or your community is used to.

As I sit typing at my computer in Massachusetts, I have no idea who you are, where you teach, or what kinds of children share your classroom with you. This book may give you some ideas, but I can assure you the reactions and work of the children in your classroom will provide you with much better feedback. Over the years, I have approached almost everything I've ever tried with a little skepticism. And I've discovered that when I throw out an untested idea to my students, they give me all the feedback I need to become a better teacher. They've taught me that I do better when I visualize how a lesson will play out and when I structure it so that each child has a chance to participate. They've taught me to let go of my preconceptions about how much and how fast they can learn and to pay attention to what they are able to do with open-ended assignments. They've taught me that getting myself organized before I come to class, a skill not native to my character, greatly enhances my ability to listen to them. These days the most important thing I do as a teacher is to concentrate on what my students are saying. So don't give up on new ideas too easily. Things rarely work perfectly the first time.

What I take from books and workshops and other teachers' classrooms is what I need. Sometimes it's a clear idea of what I *don't* want to do. Sometimes it's an organizational hint (a method for determining partners or teams, for example).

71

Sometimes it's an idea for a bulletin-board display, a system for collecting children's work, a lesson plan, a book I want to read, a way of talking to a child. I don't necessarily want to become the author of the book, the workshop presenter, or some other teacher, but I do want to make use of her or his insight and expertise.

In that spirit, I hope you will feel free to take what you need from this book, to alter it, tinker with it, embellish it, or simplify it. My greatest hope is not that you will do each of these activities but that each time you give out a homework assignment, you will think deeply about your own goals and about the children you are teaching. I hope that instead of automatically rolling their eyes as they tuck yet another arithmetic practice sheet into their backpack, your students will inadvertently let some of their enthusiasm, excitement, or curiosity escape as they deepen their understanding about the possibilities mathematics offers. I hope that you, and your students, will come to share my feeling that mathematics is fascinating, complex, challenging, interesting, and above all worthy of their intellectual engagement.

What You Can Do to Help Your Child With Math Homework This Year

- Help your child relax by putting homework in perspective.

- Talk about rules and procedures for doing homework right away.

- Identify a good place to do homework, make sure there is a generous amount of clear space, gather frequently used materials, and make sure the lighting is good.

- Help prioritize tasks. On a long-range project the teacher should provide a timetable to help your child do an acceptable amount each day toward a larger goal. Marking these smaller goals on a calendar is a wonderful way to help your child.

- Check in once or twice to ask what's left to do and how much time there is to do it.

- Model how to handle frustration by being calm and reasonable and by helping your child see that strategies and problem solving are as valuable in real life as they are in math class.

- Give help when it is needed. Determining this can be complex and tricky. And the help your child may need may not be in your repertoire of skills. Often the best help is that with organization or focus. Before you do any serious teaching, it is a good idea to talk with your child's teacher.

- Help your child refocus when he or she becomes distracted. This may mean turning off a radio or television. It may mean asking a question. It may mean delivering a glass of milk and cookie with a kind word. You'll learn to distinguish between stares of bewilderment and stares that accompany thinking.

- Set time limits—it is often better to be in bed at a decent hour than to have masterfully done homework and be too tired to pay attention the following day.

■ Verbalize how to get started—gathering appropriate materials, skimming a chapter, looking at an assignment book, jotting down ideas for a rough draft—so that your child eventually becomes independent.

■ Allow your child autonomy in figuring out when (before dinner? after dinner? all at once? in spurts?) and in what order to do assignments. Some children like to get easy, clear-cut assignments out of the way first. Some like to tackle more complicated homework and save the straightforward stuff until later. Honor your child's style and discuss it so he or she understands these patterns for tackling assignments.

■ Communicate with your child's teacher when things are not going well to find out whether both of you see the problem in the same way. Also let the teacher know when you feel homework has been serving your child well—teachers rarely hear when things are going right!

■ Point out nonessential elements (spending too much time on a cover, for example).

■ Motivate by praising, reassuring, challenging, personalizing, or editorializing. You'll know what works best for your child. Sometimes just being interested enough to look at assignments before they get packed away in backpacks communicates your support.

■ Figure out when and if taking a break is a good idea.

■ Have your child write a note to the teacher if there is something that should be shared about the way homework is going, about a specific assignment, about how homework and personal life is intersecting.

■ Don't let homework interfere with your relationship with your child. This is not meant to be a confrontational experience.

Characteristics of Good Math Homework

- It is accessible to children at many levels.

- It is interesting both to children and to any adults who may be helping.

- It is designed to provoke deep thinking.

- It is able to use concepts and mechanics as means to an end rather than as ends in themselves.

- It has problem solving, communication, number sense, and data collection at its core.

- It can be recorded in many ways.

- It is open to a variety of ways of thinking about the problem, although there may be one right answer.

- It touches upon multiple strands of mathematics, not just number.

- It is part of a variety of approaches to and types of math homework offered to children throughout the year.

Variables Associated With Homework

(adapted from Cooper 1989)

1. The *amount* of homework. How often? How long? Short term? Long term? Coordinated with other homework assignments?

2. The *purpose* of the assignment. Practice? Preparation? Extension? Integration? Improve communication with the home? Meet district policy guidelines? Foster community relations?

3. The *skills* required. Does the student need to read? Write? Memorize? Compute? Reason? Justify?

4. The degree of *individualization*. Is everybody expected to do the same thing? Do different students have different assignments? Can students create their own interpretation within broad parameters?

5. The degree of student *choice*. Is it mandatory or compulsory? Are extensions required or optional? Is the format specified or can it be completed in an alternative way?

6. The *manner* in which students are expected to work. Is it to be done independently? Is outside help permissible? Are students allowed or encouraged to work in groups?

Questions a Teacher Might Want to Ask About Homework

Below is a checklist of good questions to ask yourself before handing out a homework assignment. I staple this list in my plan book and scan it often. Sometimes I have the leisure to look at these questions while planning in the quiet of my study. Sometimes I glance at it quickly as I make up a homework assignment based not on what I thought was going to happen in class but on what actually took place. Sometimes I deal with some of these questions explicitly in the assignment: state a specific purpose or expectation, write a note to parents, give choices, talk about connections with what we are studying.

- How is this assignment related to what we are studying?

- What is the purpose of this assignment?

- How might this assignment best be carried out?

- What are my expectations for a student who has satisfactorily completed this assignment?

- Will students have access to the resources to do the assignment or an approved adaptation of it?

- Do parents have some idea of my homework philosophy and are both parents and I clear about our role in my expectations?

- Do I at least occasionally allow students to choose from several alternative approaches to a topic?

General Research Findings About Homework

(from Doyle and Barker 1990)

1. In the early school years traditional homework assignments are not very effective. Therefore, use them sparingly. *In the primary grades there is little justification for any homework.*

2. In the elementary grades devote substantial amounts of time and effort to *establishing study habits and learning skills.* This work should extend beyond traditional reading-study skills and library research. Insofar as practical, help young students become familiar with more recently developed means for storing and retrieving information computer terminals, videotapes and disks—not to be accomplished researchers but rather to feel comfortable with the variety of resources at their disposal.

3. At all levels of schooling, *allot considerably more time during the school day to independent study* and guided research. Wherever possible, use study halls and free periods as opportunities for students to pursue individual academic interests and to become proficient at a variety of research techniques.

4. *Make a basic aim of all homework learning how to learn*, not merely preparation or practice. To this end, be sure that homework assignments:

   a. Stress student initiative and freedom. Allow students to play a primary role in fashioning out-of-class work, giving them considerable latitude in determining how to accomplish the tasks chosen.

   b. Are as individualized as possible. Structure assignments taking into consideration student abilities, learning styles, and interests. Base even relatively routine assignments on knowledge of student progress and achievement, calling for individual responses within a group task.

   c. Require imagination and divergent thinking whenever possible. This does not mean that each assignment should call for an artistic response, but it should provide an opportunity for students to use imagination and creativity in identifying research topics and selecting research techniques.

d. Consider a second aim of homework learning how to teach the content or skill to someone else. The increasing emphasis on small-group and team learning, and the lifelong need for independent learning, make this a basic for all students.

5. *Be sure that the purpose of out-of-school assignments is clear* and important to students. Those who know why they are working and what they are working toward will gain greater benefit from the assignment than those who lack such knowledge. Clearly define in advance all assignments and projects, even those initiated by students.

6. Research and experience indicate that:

a. Able students are more likely to do routine homework assignments and less likely to profit by them.

b. Slower students are less likely to do routine homework assignments and more likely to profit from them.

Therefore, *assign projects, independent study, and the like to the more able and accomplish routine preparation and practice in class with slower students.*

7. *Give recognition, praise, and corrective feedback for all completed homework.* A student who has spent considerable time completing a task deserves recognition, and specific academic praise can strengthen both attitudes and diligence. Finally, students benefit from feedback on the quality of their homework. Share evaluative feedback through comments or a rating scale. Note that the amount of homework assigned to students should be adjusted to allow the teacher time to react to each individual's efforts.

8. *Keep a record of completed assignments.* Noting students' patterns of errors (weaknesses) may be more effective than giving grades, especially on independent practice activities. Viewing these assignments as practice or rehearsal, rather than the concert itself, helps keep their purpose clear.

9. Provide all students, but particularly the more able, with *frequent opportunities to engage in long-term projects that they have helped develop.*

10. Give careful consideration to demands on students' time. In the upper grades, especially, make a concerted effort to develop policies that strike a balance between the time demands of the various subjects. A most effective way to accomplish this is through the *integration of assignments*, such as a common list of supplementary readings developed by teachers of closely related subjects.

11. Recognize the importance of homework in the home-school relationship and do whatever is possible to *keep parents informed* of the kinds and amount of home study required. As the school and the home share more of the responsibility for the education in the years ahead, cooperation between home and school is even more imperative to develop a sound and sensible education program for the student.

Good Resources for Math Homework Ideas

Burns, Marilyn. *Math for Smarty Pants* and *The I Hate Mathematics Book*. The Brown Paper School Series. Little, Brown, 1974 and 1981.

Outstanding books from a great series for children. Both books have extensions consisting of mathematics activities. As wonderful for the classroom teacher as they are for parents who are looking for good enrichment activities for their children. Should be in every library and in as many classes as possible.

Childs, Leigh, et al. *Nimble with Numbers*. Grades 1/2, 2/3, 3/4, 4/5, 5/6, and 6/7. Practice Bookshelf Series. White Plains, NY: Dale Seymour, 1997 and 1998.

Games and worksheets for children to reinforce computational skills in a challenging and interesting way.

Curriculum and Evaluation Standards for School Mathematics Addenda Series, Grades 5–8. Elizabeth Phillips, *Patterns and Functions*; Barbara Reys, *Developing Number Sense in the Middle Grades*; Judith S. Zawojewski, *Dealing with Data and Chance*. Reston, VA: NCTM, 1991.

Bursting with good ideas. The number sense book is particularly good.

Fennell, Skip, and David E. Williams, compilers. *Ideas from The Arithmetic Teacher Grades 4–6*. Reston, VA: NCTM, 1986.

Includes worksheet ideas for numeration, computation with whole numbers, rational numbers, geometry, measurement, and problem solving.

McIntosh, Alistair, Barbara Reys, and Robert Reys. *NumberSENSE: Simple Effective Number Sense Experiences*. Grades 1–2, 3–4, 5–6, and 6–8. White Plains, NY: Dale Seymour, various dates.

These books are quite good at helping children figure out the magnitude of a number or relationships between numbers. Nontraditional homework!

Measuring Up: Assessments for the Intermediate Grades. Washington, DC: National Academy Press, 1993.

A collection of prototypical assessment tasks for fourth through sixth graders. Great ideas.

Problem Solving in Mathematics. The Lane County Mathematics Project. White Plains, NY: Dale Seymour, various dates.

Compilation of problem-solving strategies keyed to standard computational curriculum segments such as place value or fractions. One book for each grade level from 4 through 9 and a special book for children who do not learn as quickly as others. Not slick or beautifully illustrated, but an indispensable resource.

Wonderful Ideas. P.O. Box 64691, Burlington, VT 05406

A homegrown magazine that includes puzzles, games, mathematical ideas, and book reviews. Useful for teachers wishing to enhance their math program. Check for current subscription rates.

Good Catalogs to Have on Hand

Activity Resources Company, Inc.
P.O. Box 4875, Hayward, CA 94540
(510) 782-1300
www.activityresources.com

Creative Publications
5623 W. 115th Street, Alsip, IL 60803
(800) 624-0822
www.creativepublications.com

Critical Thinking Books & Software
P.O. Box 448, Pacific Grove, CA 93950-0448
(800) 458-4849
www.criticalthinking.com

Dale Seymour Publications/Pearson Learning
299 Jefferson Drive, Parsnippany, NJ 07054
(800) 321-3106
www.pearsonlearning.com

Delta Education
P.O. Box 3000, Nashua, NH 03061-3000
(800) 442-5444
www.delta-ed.com

Didax Educational Resources
395 Main Street, Rowley, MA 01969-1207
(800) 458-0024
www.didaxinc.com

Educators Outlet
P.O. Box 396, Timnath, CO 80547
(800) 315-2212
www.educatorsoutlet.com

ETA/Cuisenaire
500 Greenview Court, Vernon Hills, IL 60061
(800) 445-5985
www.etauniverse.com

Heinemann
88 Post Road West, P.O. Box 5007, Westport, CT 06881
(800) 793-2154
www.heinemann.com

Math Learning Center
P.O. Box 3226, Salem, OR 97302
(800) 575-8130
www.mlc.pdx.edu

Math Solutions Publications
150 Gate 5 Road, Suite 101, Sausalito, CA 94965
(800) 868-9092
www.mathsolutions.com

NASCO
901 Janesville Avenue, Ft. Atkinson, WI 53538
(800) 558-9595
www.enasco.com

National Council of Teachers of Mathematics
1906 Association Drive, Reston, VA 20191
(800) 235-7566
www.nctm.org

Summit Learning
P.O. Box 397, Ft. Collins, CO 80522
(800) 777-8817
www.summitlearning.com

Teaching Resources Center
P.O. Box 82777, San Diego, CA 92138-2777
(800) 833-8552
www.trcabc.com

In Canada

Pearson Education Canada
26 Prince Andrew Place, Don Mills, Ontario, Canada M3C 2T8
(800) 361-6128

Austin, J.D. 1979. "Homework Research in Mathematics." *School Science and Mathematics* 79 (2): 115–21.

Begley, Sharon. 1998. "Homework Doesn't Help." *Newsweek*, 30 March, 50–51.

Bresser, Rusty. 1995. *Math and Literature, Grades 4–6.* Sausalito, CA: Math Solutions Publications.

Burns, Marilyn. 1974. *Math for Smarty Pants.* The Brown Paper School Series. Boston: Little, Brown.

Canter, Lee, and Lee Hausner. 1987. *Homework Without Tears.* New York: Harper Perrenial.

Chwast, Seymour. 1993. *The Twelve Circus Rings.* New York: Harcourt Brace Jovanovich.

Clark, Clare, and Betsy Carter. 1988. *Math in Sride.* Reading, MA: Addison-Wesley Innovative.

Cooper, Harris. 1989a. "Synthesis of Research on Homework." *Educational Leadership*, November, 85–91.

———. 1989b. *Homework.* White Plains, NY: Longman.

Corno, Lyn. 1996. "Homework Is a Complicated Thing." *Educational Researcher* 25 (8): 27–30.

Developing Math Processes. 1975. Madison, WI: The Board of Regents of the University of Wisconsin System for the Wisconsin Research and Development Center for Cognitive Learning.

Doyle, Mary Anne E., and Betsy S. Barker. 1990. *Homework As a Learning Experience: What Research Says to the Teacher*. 3d ed. Washington DC: NEA Publications.

Featherstone, Helen. 1985. "What Does Homework Accomplish?" *Harvard Education Newsletter* 65 (2): 6–7.

Frasier, Deborah. 1991. *On the Day You Were Born*. San Diego and New York: Harcourt Brace.

Gill, Brian, and Steven Schlossman. 1996. "A Sin Against Childhood: Progressive Education and the Crusade to Abolish Homework, 1897–1941." *American Journal of Education* 105 (1): 27–66.

Harshmann, Marc. 1993. *Only One*. New York: Cobblehill.

Hiebert, James, and Thomas P. Carpenter. 1992. "Learning and Teaching With Understanding." In *Handbook of Research on Mathematics Teaching and Learning*, edited by Douglas Grouws. New York: MacMillan.

Hinchey, Pat. 1996. "Why Kids Say They Don't Do Their Homework." *Clearinghouse* 69 (2): 242–45.

Johnson, Judy. 1984. "Math Homework? Yes If. . . ." *The Oregon Mathematics Teacher*, September, 34–38, October, 16–20.

LaConte, Ronald. 1981. *Homework As a Learning Experience*. Washington DC: NEA Publications.

Later, Sandra. 1990. "Kids Argue for Homework." *Harvard Education Newsletter* 6 (5): 7.

Little, Jean. 1962. *Mine for Keeps*. New York: Viking Penguin.

Namioka, Lensey. 1992. *Yang the Youngest and His Terrible Ear*. New York: Dell Yearling.

O'Donnell, Elizabeth Lee. 1991. *The Twelve Days of Summer*. New York: Morrow Junior.

Pinczes, Elinor. 1995. *A Remainder of One*. Boston: Houghton Mifflin.

Points, Dana. 1989. "Homework: Your Work, Too." *Family Circle*, 5 September, 99.

Resnick, Lauren. 1987. *Education and Learning to Think*. Washington DC: Academy Press.

Stenmark, Jean Kerr, Virginia Thompson, and Ruth Cossey. 1986. *Family Math*. Berkeley, CA: Lawrence Hall of Science, University of California.

Suydam, Marilyn N. 1985. "Homework: Yes or No?" *Arithmetic Teacher* 32 (5): 56.

Third International Mathematics and Science Study. 1996–98. Chestnut Hill, MA: Boston College.

Thomas, Anne Hill. 1992. *Homework: How Effective? How Much to Assign? The Need for Clear Policies*. Monograph 36 (1). Portland: Oregon School Study Council.

Thompson, Virginia, and Karen Mayfield-Ingram. 1998. *Family Math: The Middle School Years*. Berkeley, CA: Lawrence Hall of Science, University of California.

Trivas, Irene. 1988. *Emma's Christmas*. New York: Orchard.

Tsuruda, Gary. 1994. *Putting It Together*. Portsmouth NH: Heinemann.

"What to Do About Homework." 1990. *Harvard Education Newsletter* 6 (2): 7–8.

"When Is a Tablespoon Not a Tablespoon?" 1999. *Gourmet Magazine* (Good Living), September, 32.

Wickett, Maryann. 1997. "Investigating Probability and Patterns With the Thirteen Days of Halloween." *Teaching Children Mathematics* 4 (2): 90–94.

Winerup, Michael. 1999. "Homework Bound." *New York Times Education Life*, 3 January, 28–40.

Wirtz, Robert. 1976. *Banking on Problem Solving*. Washington DC: Curriculum Development Associates.

Xu, Jianzhong, and Lyn Corno, 1998a. "Doing Third-Grade Homework." *Teachers College Record* 100 (2): 402–36.

———. 1998b. "Homework and Personal Responsibility." Paper presented at the annual meeting of the American Educational Research Association, San Diego, California.

Young, Ed. 1992. *Seven Blind Mice*. New York: Philomel.

Young, Sharon L. 1990. Ideas column. *Arithmetic Teacher* 38 (2): 24–34.

———. 1991. Ideas column. *Arithmetic Teacher* 38 (8): 26–33.